SIXTY-ONE

LARRY JOHNSON

Lost Lake Folk Art

SHIPWRECKT BOOKS PUBLISHING COMPANY

Rushford, Minnesota

Front cover: Doug Freeman's sculpture *Walking with Birds*,
photo by Gary Melom.
Cover design by Shipwreckt Books

ISBN-10: 0-9968909-0-4
ISBN-13: 978-0-9968909-0-8

Photos

Dedication

This book is for Elaine Wynne, my most wonderful partner in every way since 1982. We've been together in love and in blending families as parents and grandparents. We've also worked together in many arenas as storyteller activists, building bridges, healing old wounds, and walking in the woods.

We slept outside as lovers by Lake Michigan, waves and whippoorwills whispering yes, and we slept outside at Chaco Canyon, a mysterious star moving above to bless our marriage. In Glastonbury, England, one of the many places King Arthur is buried, we stood strong together as we were nearly blown off the Tor Hill. We swam with the dolphins, rode high above New Mexico in a hot air balloon, and we sit in silent grief each day over the violence and corruption pervading this beautiful world. We share the commitment to nonviolence, and to finding and telling the important stories the culture just wants to bury and ignore.

Elaine's version of the old Irish tale, *The Peddlar of Ballaghadreen,* is the best I've ever heard. Often, when I have to do something really hard, I get it done only because I remember this from the *Peddlar*: "I don't know how the tired old man made it to Dublin, but I think it must have been by just putting one foot ahead of the other".

Elaine drove the supply car for the 61-mile hike, and she walked small parts of it. She walks a lot; just not extremes like 61 and 70-mile hikes. She is most known for walking into the middle of crucial situations to straighten them out or to make them go. I applaud her for her ongoing, forever, concern for family, and most currently for her long walk, and fight, to make EMDR Trauma Therapy available to veterans.

ONE

In 1961, as a junior high athlete, I did the 50-mile hike, promoted by the Kennedy Administration at the time to encourage physical fitness. When I turned 50 in 1996, I intended to reproduce the feat to promote re-election for our great Senator Paul Wellstone. I was instead too sick to crawl, after prolonged exposure to mold and other toxins in a school treating teachers and children like Vietnam veterans exposed to Agent Orange.

Quite spontaneously, I decided to do a 61-mile hike on my 61st birthday in 2007, encouraged that time around to promote strategies for fewer wars, fewer veterans and better care for them when they return home. In addition, my 61-mile hike plan included a mechanism intended to complete funding for the Peace Garden by Lake Harriet in Minneapolis.

1. Heading out on Highway 61 with Tyler.

My grandson Tyler elected to do the hike with me over two days instead of one because we would be covering 11 miles more than I had hiked in 1961, and of course because I was 46 years older. We also walked for Tyler's great uncle, Kale Solberg, whose name is etched on the Vietnam Memorial Wall in Washington.

On August 9, 2007, at 6:10 a.m., we got on bus #61 in downtown Minneapolis, right at the corner where the light rail takes you to the Mall of America. The Mall, built on the spot where the Minnesota Twins started playing at Metropolitan Stadium in 1961, is also where I began my first 50-mile hike nearly five decades earlier. We took bus #61 to Highway 61 and headed north on the famous road that follows the Mississippi from northern Minnesota to the Gulf of Mexico. At 6:10 that evening, we brought together members of Veterans for Peace and the VFW for a ceremony to honor the sacrifice of service members at the Veterans Memorial in Lindstrom, Minnesota. My grandfather and uncle, both veterans, are buried in Lindstrom, as is my father, who died at age 61.

My mother, whom I believe did her best to prevent me from being drafted during the Vietnam War, also lies at rest in Lindstrom, the town where she grew up. On August 10, we left again at 6:10 a.m., crossing the bridge into Wisconsin, then heading south to Osceola, where we crossed back into Minnesota. It was a 95-degree day, but we drank a lot of water, walked in shade as much as possible, and eventually crossed the Lake Street Peace Bridge for a 6:10 Ceremony of Peace at the Minneapolis Midtown Market, established to reflect fair trade and cultures from around the world.

TWO

Growing up conservative Protestant in the 50s, my neighborhood friends and I were taught to think of the Catholic Kennedy Presidency as a disaster. After all, the Pope was the antichrist. Still, we were inspired by the charismatic leader who said, "Ask not what your country can do for you, but what you can do for your country."

My dad mapped out a route for us in the car. All of my friends planned to go on the 50-mile hike, *for the President, and for our Country*. I had, for several years before 1961, knocked on doors weekly to collect my paper route money, so I was familiar with excuses. But never had I heard the excuses I heard when I knocked on doors to wake up friends to walk with me, as patriots.

I ended up taking the challenge alone, not even telling my parents of my solo hike because I was afraid they might try to stop me. Leaving the baseball stadium near my home, I headed south on old Cedar Avenue, walked west somewhere south of Lakeville, and headed home down the roadbed of I35W freeway, which was under construction in 1961. Halfway out, my body desperately wanted me to use my emergency dime to call for a ride, but that wasn't even an option. Intent on beating a Marine I'd heard about who completed the hike in 8 ½ hours, I kept walking. The hike took me 13½ hours, but I finished proud – not ready to do it again soon, but proud.

Most of the promotion that influenced me to take a 50-mile hike focused on Marines finishing the course, but somehow I never processed the idea that the hike grew out of an extreme military test. For me it was just one more physical challenge, and my ongoing athletic training enabled me to finish well under the 50 miles in less than 20 hours, the standard for Marines. True, I wasn't wearing a fifty-pound pack required by the Marine Corps, but I only weighed 89 pounds.

The event put me in line, when I was drafted, to pass the army basic training PT test so far ahead of everyone else, they gave me an early pass from Fort Sam Houston to San Antonio. I was rewarded with a Sunday in town. In full dress uniform, I went by myself, making it the loneliest day of my life up to that moment.

WRESTLERS FINISH UNDEFEATED YEAR

The PJHS wrestling squad finished off an undefeated season last Friday night when they out- pinned and out-wrestled the Hopkins boys here at 4:00.

Individual scores were

95 lbs.	Larry Johnson won, 8-3
103 lbs.	Dick Spangler won, pin
112 lbs.	Jim Rasicot won, pin
120 lbs.	Doug McComb won, pin
127 lbs.	Dennis Rassmusen lost, 4-6
133 lbs.	Jim Meritt lost, pin
138 lbs.	Glen Wien won, 5-3
145 lbs.	Gary Seimes lost, 3-0
155 lbs.	Lenny Cox tied, 2-2
Heaveyweight	Mike Pauling won, pin

Not only has the team come through the season undefeated, but three team members have won every one of their events during the season —Larry Johnson, Dick Spangler, and Jim Rasicot. Congratulations to them, the team, and Coach Anderson for their fine work.

2. Junior High Wrestling 1961.

THREE

"You are a force for peace and for nature!"

Stephen J. Gates, Vietnam Veteran, Artist, Frequent Fellow Walker

Number 61 on the Periodic Table is assigned to the highly radioactive element *Promethium*, named for a Greek god Prometheus who created the human race from clay. He then defied the bigger gods by stealing fire from Mount Olympus and giving it to humans. Zeus punished Prometheus by chaining him to a rock where every day an eagle eats his liver and every night, being an immortal god, he regenerates. Having spent the 50s, hiding under desks as protection from atom bombs that had already vaporized two cities, I think we may have defied the gods by creating nuclear weapons.

After I finished walking 61 miles and obsessing about the number 61, people asked, "So what are you doing next year? Walking 62 miles?" It was never my intention to become mechanical. The mystical experience leading to the 61-mile hike was rather one-of-a-kind, starting with an overpowering feeling, almost an inaudible voice, saying you must do this to finish the funding for the Peace Garden. I have each year since then, done some sort of symbolic, shorter walk, each emerging from a place of intuition.

I did listen to my sister Karol, who said I should do 70 miles on my 70th birthday, because the Sixty-one story said my dad died when he was 61. "Mom was 70 when she died," Karol said right away. "It's only right you do 70 miles when you're 70."

Almost immediately, I began making plans, thinking it would take me three days, because it's further again, and I'd be older still, and it would be a statement about nuclear proliferation, cancer and radiation.

We were told nuclear power would improve life, but we're rarely allowed to think carefully about the connection

3. Walking with windmills.

between radiation and diseases like cancer. Most of us have no idea that nuclear power plants are considered so dangerous that private insurers won't cover them. We pay property insurance bills to protect us from most things. Then we pay taxes to protect us from disasters at the nuclear power plant. Most have no idea, unless they're compulsive and read the entire policy. The powerful, clever nuclear lobby even has some environmentalists, generally in favor of healthy clean energy, fighting wind power to save the birds. Some birds are killed by wind generator blades, but the missing piece is an astronomically larger number are killed by flying into house windows. I imagine nuclear power is cleaner than coal or oil, as claimed, but it's far less clean than wind or solar. The taxpayer funded insurance policy has been an enormous hidden subsidy from the start.

The 70-mile hike will end up at Lake Pepin, the place William Cullen Bryant said all artists should visit once a year. Bryant also wrote *To a Waterfowl*, saying, "He, who from zone to zone, guides thru the boundless sky thy certain flight, in the long way that I must trace alone, will lead my steps aright."

I don't know if Bryant was referring to cranes, who love wetlands, but I defer to the International Crane Foundation, near Baraboo, Wisconsin, where biologists years ago observed cranes, worldwide, facing extinction. Like a modern Noah's Ark, they began bringing different species of cranes, two by two, to Baraboo, where they worked on breeding and strengthening them, then returning them to their native areas if the locals would work on improving environmental conditions for the cranes.

From the beginning, the ICF premise was, "Cranes are a bit like the canary in the coal mine. If the environment is bad, the cranes are affected first, but it's not doing the people any good either." **I'll walk to that.**

FOUR

Virtually everyone has heard JFK's "Ask not what your country can do for you; no, ask what you can do for your country." Few know he also said, "War will end when the conscientious objector has the same status in the culture, as does the warrior."

Franz Jagerstatter, a Catholic farmer in Germany, was executed on my birthday, three years before I was born, for refusing to join Hitler's army. He said something to the effect that, "*Taking part in Hitler's world would violate everything about my faith in God.*"

My church said, "Read the Bible daily." So I read the Good Book cover to cover three times before I graduated high school. There were things that troubled me, like the command to go into all the world to save the heathen, at the same time as church leaders said, it was God's will to kill the godless Communists before they destroyed our religious freedom. I had questions, but accepted the answers of the only sincere spiritual leaders I knew. That was until I encountered the historic peace churches. The Quakers were liberal, but the Mennonites and Church of the Brethren had the same literal Bible theology I grew up with. They refused, however, to kill, even in war, because that's how the early Christians lived for the first 300 years. Some kept this belief even after Constantine made Christianity a state church and got theologians to engineer the Just War Theory.

I have a University minor in history and political science, not because I was initially interested in those topics, but because I spent 3 intense years taking every course I could to prove or disprove this difference on what it meant to follow the Bible literally. My conscientious objection statement is dated March 1970, six months before I was actually drafted, and it's in the vein of John Prine's wonderful 1971 song *Flag Decal* that proclaims "Jesus don't like killin' no matter what the reason is for."

When I went before the draft board, I signed the blank that said, if drafted, I would be a medic, but not carry a weapon or deliberately take lives. I had noble ideals about getting people back home where they belonged, but years later I realized the major reason I did that, rather than stay out and do alternative service, was to be less of an affront to my parents who would have to continue to live around their opinionated church friends. Unfortunately, it made little or no difference. Despite the fact I served as a medic in the military, I was judged severely for refusal to kill the godless Communists.

FIVE

Elaine and I have walked and used public transit all over the world, because it pollutes less and is better economically than even a hybrid. We share one hybrid, and she drove that on the 61 Mile Hike as the water, supplies, and emergency vehicle. My parents lived similarly, and by upper grade school, I was taking the bus, alone, downtown to see the doctor. However, my benign military service amped up an activism about public transit.

When I graduated as a medic, they said we were going to Germany for three months and then on to Vietnam, which, of course, has a quite different public transit system than Europe. I never did end up in Vietnam, but I also didn't tell my first wife the part about three months in Germany. She was already distraught that I'd been drafted. We were on a two year waiting list for adoption, and the system, in its infinite wisdom, pushed us to the top of the list and rewarded us with a baby girl as I was shipping out to Germany. I spent money we didn't have to bring my family over, thinking, "I'll be on orders to Nam in a short time. What if this is the last time I see them?" Drafted personnel with families could not live on base, so I worked the whole time, riding bike to the little clinic at Wiley Kaserne, near New Ulm, where we found an apartment next to the train station. When I was off duty, we used an amazing public transit system to travel *Southern Europe on Five Diapers a Day*, and I came home determined to make our system work like the one in Europe. I served on the Advisory Committee on Transit in the 70s, and I've always maintained office space on whichever bus I was writing on.

Of course there's also the intent to make up in any way I can for participating in Barry Sanders' claim, in "The Green Zone: The Environmental Costs of Militarism", that the U.S. military is the biggest polluter on the planet. As a medic, the only one who had driven school bus back home, I drove a two-ton supply truck every other week to the hospital in Augsburg. Though our general training included the absolute necessity to refuse an unlawful order, I had intense fear that I'd be ordered to drive the truck around at the end of the year to burn gas so the allocation would stay the same. For me, wasting taxpayer money deliberately would be an unlawful order. Yet I knew if I refused, I would be in enormous trouble, with a wife and child to support. That order never happened either.

Six

The summer of the 61-mile hike, I walked 17 miles three times, from my home, in each case to some symbolic event happening at our State Capitol, St. Paul. It was, of course, training, but also testing to make sure I hadn't committed to something foolish. On Memorial Day, I was on the phone with my grandson Tyler, reminding him about the upcoming hike and why I was walking this day. Suddenly he asked, "When is that hike again?" I told him, and he said, "I'm going to see if I can get off work and walk with you." I could hear in his voice that it was a done deal, which was wonderful because Tyler happened to be the same age I was in 1961.

In June I walked to a massive World War Two commemoration, spread all over the Capitol grounds. As I wandered the displays, I ran into a young woman who knew my long history of starting children's gardens.

"I'm here with my grandma," she said. "We're remembering my grandpa. He died, but he was in World War Two." She paused before adding, "You'll appreciate this. My grandpa was stationed in the South Pacific, and the men in his company got tired of eating C-rations. They wanted fresh grown food, but all the soil was beach sand. Somebody had the idea to organize and get everyone they knew back home to mail boxes of good soil, which they did. When they had enough, they mixed soil from home into a spot on the beach where they could grow their own food."

The woman was right. I appreciated the anecdote a lot. I had a garden behind the Gasthaus, across the highway from the base where I served as a medic. I also remember the anticipation of mail-call. Putting them together, gardening and mail-call, made it one of the best war stories I've heard.

On July 4, walking thru Minneapolis on the way to the celebration in St. Paul, I crossed the small bridge over I-35W freeway, just before I-35W crosses over the Mississippi River. At the base of the I-35W bridge grew a profusion of flowers that reminded me so much of white poppies, the rest of my day became a blur. As soon as I got home, I reviewed *In Flanders Fields* by Canadian Lieutenant-Colonel John McCrae.

4. Tending a garden plot given to me by the owner of the *gasthaus*, across the highway from our army base near Neu Ulm, Germany.

McCrae, a military surgeon, wrote the famous poem, in May 1915, during World War One, at the 2nd Battle of Ypres. Following a horrendous seventeen-day stretch of tending to wounded and dying, which included the death of his friend, Lieutenant Alexis Helmer, McCrae penned this iconic war poem:

In Flanders fields the poppies blow
Between the crosses, row on row,
That mark our place; and in the sky
The larks, still bravely singing, fly
Scarce heard amid the guns below.

We are the Dead. Short days ago
We lived, felt dawn, saw sunset glow,
Loved and were loved, and now we lie
In Flanders fields.

One month later, just a week before my 61-mile hike with Tyler, the I-35W bridge collapsed during rush hour in the Twin Cities, a disaster many believed happened because we were too long focused on blowing up bridges overseas rather than building or maintaining them here at home.

SEVEN

I started telling goofy campfire stories when I was running summer camps in the late 60s. At some point, I observed that stories with some inherent message were the best way to teach. My earliest formed stories, modelled pretty closely on how we grew up, were about *The World's Holiest Backyard,* where, "Your backyard is holy if you dig lots of holes and learn to care wholly for others." My dad, a remodeler and home builder, taught us to build forts the way real houses were built, and we secretly dug basements under them.

While playing backyard baseball, we dug holes on every base from sliding-in. We dug holes to bury pirate treasures, beloved cats, and more. My parents clearly believed in "Spare the **sod** and spoil the child."

One night we listened in horror through the upstairs heating vent as some *friends* from church berated them, "Your yard is an eyesore. You're too lax with your children. You know the scriptures say, "*Spare the rod and spoil the child*.""

According to those same friends, the Bible also said "no dancing." For a long time, as an adult, I felt disgusted to think my first act of standing up for what I believed was to resign as a high school class officer because the main job of junior class officers was to plan the senior prom. When I finally made it to a high school reunion, I was thankfully remembered as an exceptional athlete, not an anti-dancer. Then I remembered the stand I took as a nine-year-old, when the Biblical rod appeared after the eyesore incident. The actual implement for parental violence was more horrifying than overhearing neighborhood dissension. As the older sibling, I waited for the right moment, took the stick outside and broke it into enough small pieces to start a good fire.

My parents never said a word, and any thought of sticks for beating children into obedience vanished. We reverted back to the caring, somewhat stern talks. I'm not saying my parents were perfect. I'm just saying they only believed the rhetoric of the church when it didn't violate their own God-given moral compass.

EIGHT

The following anecdote is pretty true, but some of the facts have been exaggerated to protect the innocent. There was a gopher in our backyard named Seymour, and I'm sorry to say that in 1954 we obeyed orders to push a garden hose down the gopher hole to kill him for digging up the yard. In desperation, the gopher grabbed his end of the hose and blew a bugle call that amplified thru the plumbing system, causing a sound explosion that flattened weaker sheds and knocked out windows throughout the neighborhood. In the spirit of Alfred Nobel, who created the Nobel Peace Prize after becoming wealthy selling explosives, the gopher redeemed himself. Hooking recycled garden hose to outside faucets all around the neighborhood, Seymour nightly calmed unruly children by broadcasting over Radio H-O-S-E *Theater in the Ground.* Caring bedtime stories travelled thru the hose and indoor pipes so children could hear them coming out the bathtub drain or washbowl.

A few years after Seymour's death, someone sliding vociferously into third base threw up enough dirt to unearth a buried coffee can. Inside, sealed in a bread bag, were what came to be known as THE DEAD SEYMOUR SCROLLS, the last writings of this repentant gopher. At the time we had little understanding of what he was talking about, but I reproduce some of the sayings here, now that I have some comprehension of the wisdom left by this wise creature of the Earth:

> God so loved the world that he gave his only Son, that his followers might build magnificent churches, and their payments have eternal life.

War separates soldiers from family so they can separate others from their own.

The blue ribbon for whoever wins the arms race will be laid on a pile of debris.

Refusing to go to war puts one in trouble with one's own country. Going puts one in jeopardy with someone else's.

Even geese fly south in peace sign formation.

NINE

Storytelling can be used to lie to and hurt people, but it's highest calling is to generate intimacy and bring people together. I'd always spent time with my dad, but the year he died we spent considerably more time together. We decided to finish an old project to get all his stories on audiotape. Years earlier, when I had suggested doing this, he said, "I'm not a storyteller. You're a storyteller. Your Grandpa Johnson was a storyteller. People came from all over the neighborhood to hear him tell his own stories, and the ones Will Rogers did on the radio."

It took me a while to realize what Dad meant, because he told stories all the time, some for fun and some for life lessons. However, he wouldn't get up in front of an audience to perform. He thought he wasn't a storyteller, but he was.

Sometimes, when I went out to the house to record his stories, Dad was in such pain I would ask, "Dad, are you sure you want to do this today?"

He'd say, "I want to get it done," and I'd start the recorder.

I'd say, "Tell me the one about . . ."

Dad would talk until he fell asleep, with the same look of peace and relief as when they gave him liquid morphine.

Of course, eventually the one-on-one storytelling got us into talking about things that should have been talked about years earlier, but we'd never discussed. "I never understood that decision you made during Vietnam," he said one time, "about being a conscientious objector. Even the Bible says there shall be wars and rumors of wars."

I thought for a second before replying, "Dad, that's a statement of the way things are. It doesn't mean its right to participate in making wars happen."

Dad paused, then told me a story I think no one had ever heard.

> "When they bombed Pearl Harbor, I went down to enlist, and they wouldn't take me. I'd fallen off a ladder that year and had a slight concussion. They rejected me."

I could feel the pain, perhaps worse than the pain caused by the cancer. His inability to do what everyone else was doing had tainted his life with the false idea he wasn't a real man.

> "I saw an ad for taking a welding course in Berkeley so you could work on the war ships. I'd always wanted to learn to weld, so I went. When we graduated, they gave me a rivet gun and told me to stand by this ship and make it look like I was working. I couldn't believe it. I did this for a few days and couldn't stand lying. I wasn't enlisted, so they couldn't hold me. I quit, hitchhiked home and went back to work."

That's pretty much how he told it, making no value judgments. Again, I felt his pain at being asked to violate what he had taught me, the value of an honest, hard day's work. He couldn't bring himself to use the term *Defense Contractor Fraud*, or to say, "Something was rotten with this," but it felt like he was telling me as best he could, "Well, maybe I can sort of understand what you did. I mean, even in a war as pure as World War Two, not everything was on the up and up."

TEN

The most striking part of military training for me came in Geneva Conventions class.

"There are rules to war?" I reacted.

We were taught, with great authority, that we were to abide by these rules, though "they (the enemy) do not."

The internationally sanctioned rules, in brief, state that it is a war crime to kill civilians, or to torture captured enemy combatants.

I don't remember any mention of My Lai and the massacre of as many as 500 Vietnamese civilians by U.S. soldiers on March 16, 1968, although I had paid attention to the report when it appeared briefly in the news before I was drafted. Years later, I met Hugh Thompson, the Army helicopter pilot who saw American troops mowing down old men, women, and children in the little Vietnamese village, My Lai. Thompson viewed this as gross violation of the Geneva Conventions he, like me, had learned about in Basic Training.

Thompson landed his helicopter, asking his crew, Larry Colburn and Glenn Andreotta, to cover for him as he got out and ordered soldiers from the 23rd – Americal – Infantry Division to quit firing at civilians. We would have never heard about this, as there was an immediate effort to cover it up, but a former helicopter door gunner from the 11th Infantry Brigade, Sp-5 Ronald L. Ridenhour, flew over the destruction at My Lai a few days after the massacre. When efforts to report the incident to his superiors failed, Ridenhour informed 30 members of the U.S. Congress in a March 1969 letter. Because of Ridenhour's efforts, the event was reported and investigated.

Captain Hugh Thompson was harassed the rest of his time in the military for doing what he was taught to do by

Geneva Conventions training – to report violations. The main thing used against him was his threat to shoot soldiers if they did not stop killing Vietnamese civilians, as he felt they might not listen otherwise. Thirty years after My Lai, Hugh Thompson and his former crew members were awarded the Soldier's Medal, the Army's highest recognition of heroism not involving conflict with an enemy. Subsequently, Thompson threw the medal away. In 1999, he received the Peace Abbey Courage of Conscience Award, and later returned to Vietnam to meet with Mỹ Lai survivors.

I walked at age 62 for Hugh Thompson because that was his age when he died.

Those willing to admit it know there were many such incidents during Vietnam, much of it to up body counts so officers could be promoted. It's not necessarily standard practice, but ***war is hell***. The same thing happened at the end of World War One, when deliberate, "move to the next rank" killing amped up before the actual signing of the Armistice. We also know that since developing the ability to drop bombs from planes on other cities, the percentage of civilians killed in warfare has climbed from very small numbers to something like ninety percent.

The book "Bombing Civilians" by Yuki Tanaka and Marilyn Young points out that we prosecuted the Germans after World War Two for their general aggression and activities during the Holocaust, but did not prosecute them for illegally bombing European cities. Had the U.S. made that an issue, the U.S. would have been equally culpable. I'm not arguing here against legitimate defense. I'm saying let's start basing our defense on the truth.

If there's a war and, horrible as it is, 100,000 people die, 15 of them civilians, I suppose you could call those 15 noncombatants collateral damage. When do we decide, however, that our integrity is stretched by twisting the story to read that ninety percent of the casualties of modern warfare are mere unfortunate mistakes, civilians in the wrong place at the wrong time?

ELEVEN

This might be faster than the speed of life, but I believe we have high-level confusion over the difference between force and violence. When I stood before the draft board to defend my conscientious objection statement, their main question was, "What if a bunch of guys started to rape your wife? What would you do?" Their intimidating tone and body language implied that if I would do anything at all, I didn't believe in the non-violence I was professing. I hadn't thought this through. I felt paralyzed, and have no memory of how I answered. I had only prepared myself with an articulate, somewhat naïve belief-statement based on the literal words of the Bible about killing, accompanied by how those teachings were followed historically by the disciples of Jesus. A respected church leader stood beside me before the draft board, but neither of us knew how to respond to a culture that believes, "If they do something bad, kill 'em."

I removed the intent to deliberately take life when I signed on as a conscientious objector, but what is the force that stops wrongdoing? At the time, still caught in the importance of following the literal Biblical truth, I looked for Bible support and couldn't find it. What I did find was a story in the Hindu Upanishads that gave me some guidance and direction. It goes something like this:

> A poisonous snake, in the habit of
> striking and killing those passing by,
> lunged to bury its venom in a Holy
> Man. "Stop," cried the holy one.
> "Don't you know it's wrong to take
> another's life?" Awed by the power of
> the man's words and essence, the

snake vowed to follow his teachings. A few days later the Holy Man again encountered the snake. This time the poor snake was extremely battered and bruised. "What happened to you?" cried the Holy Man.

The snake replied, "I stopped killing, like you said, and they started beating me up."

With intense kindness, the teacher said, "My child. I said you must not take another's life. I never said you shouldn't ***hiss*** to frighten them away if they try to hurt you or others."

Most of us will never become foreign policy leaders, but we can be citizens devoted to the sacredness of all life, diligently dredging up stories of nonviolent force to be adapted and applied at higher levels. The reality is that far fewer Holocaust victims were saved by our military intervention than by brave individuals who secreted people out of the camps to freedom. Most of those courageous persons we'll never know, because the culture mainly wishes to define courage through acts of violence.

Also, my high school wrestling experience taught me some things about taking people down forcefully without killing them, and now, after all these years, I think I found it in the Bible. Back when I made my decision to declare myself a conscientious objector, people who had been my friends and colleagues argued angrily, "Jesus used violence when he tipped over the moneychanger's tables. That proves it is right to go to war when it's a just cause."

That is where I finally found the Biblical ***force*** to resist the evil that is war. Jesus was angry about people using the temple to take advantage of worshippers' needs to make animal sacrifices. He tipped over their sales tables, saying, "This is God's House. You've made it a den of thieves." But he didn't kill anyone. In the same way that some people spin the moneychanger story into Jesus' justification for war, I now see it as finding the force to overturn and disrupt the ***tables*** of those defense contractors who profit from perpetuating misery and death around the world, too often even selling to both sides in a conflict.

TWELVE

I've always been interested in the idea of athletic competition replacing the violence of war, but it's problematic. Roger Maris hit 61 home runs in 1961, and broke the long standing record of 60 set by Babe Ruth in 1927. The problem was he did it as a Yankee, and the New York fans and sportswriters couldn't accept this was done by the clean-living farm boy from Minnesota and North Dakota. Mickey Mantle, the flamboyant Yankee hero was supposed to break the record. Surely he was hampered by his playboy, drunken lifestyle, but that, together with his baseball skill, was exactly what made him darling of the media.

5. Walking out to throw the first pitch at St. Paul Saints game.

Seventy years earlier, a Frenchman, Pierre de Coubertin, started promoting physical education, first as a way to stay healthier, then to make his country's soldiers better able to win wars. That led him full circle to reestablish the ancient Olympic Games as a worldwide competition in 1896. His idea was to demonstrate international prowess of individual nations athletically rather than on the battlefield, a better way to show, "My dad's tougher than your dad." So far, this hasn't worked out as a substitute for war. General media coverage deemed it naïve for that reason. Rather than promoting and giving the idea prominence in the sports section, the press implied it was foolish, not unlike diminishing Roger Maris because he wasn't as exciting as Mickey Mantle.

Muhammed Ali, aka Cassius Clay, was an exciting and popular sports celebrity in the 60s until he refused to be inducted into the Army in April 1967, declaring on religious grounds that he would not fight people in Vietnam who never told him which restaurants, drinking fountains and restrooms he could or could not use. Not only was he stripped of his heavyweight championship, but the Ali was convicted of draft evasion, sentenced to five years in prison, fined $10,000 and banned from boxing for three years. It is true that Ali used his boxing notoriety to make a political statement at a time when sports heroes and celebrities went to war because it was the patriotic thing to do. It's also true that among the movie war heroes promoting patriotism were people like John Wayne and Sylvester Stallone. Neither of them were drafted, nor did either of them enlist to fight in their respective wars.

The Olympics idea could work as an alternative to war, but the media would have to decide that fighting to demonstrate speed and strength could sell as many ads as fighting to the death; also that telling the truth about illicit weapons manufacture and distribution is more important to freedom than bigger profits.

THIRTEEN

There's an old story about a Peace Corps Volunteer who brought a TV set to a remote village to show people how and why to use it. When he returned months later, the villagers had unplugged the TV and turned it to face the wall.

"What's wrong?" asked the volunteer, "Did it break?"

"No," said the villagers, "we don't need it. We've got a storyteller."

The American said, "Wait a minute. That TV can tell you a lot more stories than any old storyteller. Here, let's get it going again."

The villagers stopped him, saying, "No, we know your TV box knows lots of stories, but it doesn't matter because our storyteller knows us."

In the 90s, George Gerbner, Dean of the Annenberg School of Communication at the University of Pennsylvania until 1989, organized the Cultural Environment Movement. He gathered leaders from social service, communications, environmental, legal, religious and many other circles to look for stories that weren't being told by major media. My wife Elaine and I were honored to be asked to represent the national storytelling community on the founding board with the rallying cry: THE STORIES MUST BE IN THE HANDS OF PEOPLE WITH SOMETHING TO TELL, NOT JUST LARGE CORPORATIONS WITH SOMETHING TO SELL.

A few years ago, the longtime CEO of a major local defense contractor died. His obituary, recorded in the major media, said he prided himself on telling protesters, "We sell weapons because if people can't defend themselves, you get the aggression of a Hitler during World War Two." The TVs of the world tell lots of stories like that, but a good storyteller, who knows the people, not just the big corporation paying him, tells a different story. He or she says, "Yes, but Hitler got most of his weapons, in the 30s, from companies in America and other Allied Nations."

Whenever someone says, "I'm in favor of working for nonviolent negotiation of international conflict," someone else steps up and shouts, belligerently, "Oh, yeah. How would you stop Hitler with that?"

11-20-98
Dear Larry,
I loved that story.
I liked the way
you told the story.
It was like it was
really true. And it felt
like I was in it.
I loved the whole thing
Thank you Larry.
By Calvin Raymond

6. A wonderful letter thanking me for having something to tell, not just something to sell.

A big part of the answer is, "Don't let your own people profit from arming Hitler in the first place."

FOURTEEN

I read the Koran while still in high school. Admittedly, I read it to demonstrate to myself how wrong it was, but I was encouraged to read outside my existing belief system by Mr. Kuzma, an outstanding World History teacher. Later, inspired by "On Liberty" and John Stuart Mill's plea to allow the clash of differing opinions so that truth can emerge, I read Adolph Hitler's "Mein Kampf". I was stunned to find that it sounded like other religious tracts I had read growing up. I could have been reading a Billy Graham sermon, except for the places where he went into, "the Jews did this, and the Jews are this … therefore it is the will of God that we exterminate the Jews."

It would be easy to stand back and think, "Well, that's so horrendous, people couldn't possibly believe it. Surely, if they knew he believed in exterminating Jews, they'd protest." Some did of course, and paid dearly for it; but the majority went along, either out of fear or because they agreed, even if weakly.

Ever since reading Hitler, I've felt extremely cautious when someone says, "It's the will of God."

I have a copy of an episode of *The Waltons*, popular from 1971-1981, where the townsfolk are up in arms because John Boy, now a young adult, is publishing "Mein Kampf" in his newspaper. John Boy's point was to inform people about what Hitler was saying, but the protest escalated to a massive burning of German books to show the young Walton how wrong he is. John attends the burning. Horrified, he pulls a book from the fire, hands it to an older woman he knows to be German and begs her to read it.

Frightened, yet courageous at the same time, she opens to the first page, and reads, "Am Anfang schuf Gott Himmel und Erde."

At John Boy's insistence, she translates, "In the Beginning, God created the Heavens and the Earth," to reveal the opening passage from the Book of Genesis in a German Bible the militant Christians had tried to burn.

After my mom died, I found the letters I sent my parents during the time I was in the military. In with those letters was a newspaper article Mom had saved, written by a conservative Christian father who had lost his son in Vietnam. The grieving father said, with great passion and detail, "I don't believe it was the will of God for my son to die in Vietnam. As a people and a nation we have sinned and perpetuated too many ways for war to continue. It needs to stop."

Thank God for people like that soldier's father, and for Mr. Kuzma, and for the producers of *The Waltons*; and also for my mom for saving that article.

FIFTEEN

When I was in grade school, my grandfather, a World War One veteran, gave me a pocketknife. He taught me to keep it sharp and use it safely as a tool for whittling, cleaning fish, cutting rope and more. When I was in junior high, my dad gave me a boy scout knife, which added a can opener, bottle opener and screw driver to my little *pocket toolbox*. That knife served me well, especially when I ran trip camps for several years before I got drafted. When I arrived at Fort Knox for induction processing, the military confiscated my dad's gift, saying it was a dangerous weapon. The next day, those of us who were conscientious objectors, peeled potatoes for the mess hall while most went out for weapons training, many of them blustering, "I can't wait to get out there to kill a gook."

As a medic in Germany, I frequented the Ulm, Germany, hardware store window for about six months trying to decide whether I could justify spending $10 for a Swiss Army Knife, bright red, with a cross insignia. It was a Boy Scout knife-plus, adding a small saw blade, scissors, tweezers, toothpick, corkscrew and more. I finally purchased it and used it as a wonderful tool for the years I ran camps after I got out of the Army.

Later, there came a time when I had to discontinue my practice of carrying a pocketknife, because it was considered a dangerous weapon in schools and other places I appeared to tell stories. It was frustrating to be without a needed tool, so I sometimes took it, in my suitcase, when we traveled. Early after the events of September 11, 2001, when hijacked planes crashed into the World Trade Center, I forgot to remove the knife from my suitcase before we boarded a plane. Afterward, airline security owned my knife.

When I quit working for the Minneapolis school district in 2006, I did a lot of short term project work. I went through six or seven background checks the first year. At one point, I said, "I just had this done. Can't the results be shared?"

The reply was, "Don't worry. You don't have to pay for it."

So I said, "I know, but you do," aware I was talking to the same kind of low budget nonprofit operation I had worked for much of my life.

At this moment, I'm struck by the fact we've been confiscating pocketknives for years, as well as raising security on mostly benign civilians. Yet, no matter how many mass shootings in public places, we lack the political will to do background checks on people buying guns.

My grandfather, who gave me the pocketknife, was a hunter. Under the bench at the breakfast table cove, he kept a toy rifle for us to play with. We had to ask for it, and one time I did what children, trained by culture and media, too often do. I pointed the toy at my grandfather and shouted, "Bang!" With a stern but still loving look, he took the gun. "Don't you ever point even a toy gun at a person. You only point a gun at an animal if you intend to kill it, and then you eat what you kill."

In 1995, the first time we visited with one of my Swedish relatives, a farmer and hunter, he said, "I don't get how you do guns in America. I would pay huge fines if I were caught with my hunting rifles loaded and not locked up. I hunt for a lot of our food, but I am required by law to be extremely careful."

I don't get it either. I don't get how we do guns, or pocket knives, in America.

SIXTEEN

After World War Two, when developers mowed down everything outside big cities to build rows of suburban houses, my dad built homes one or two at a time. He left the woods on a lot standing, and, in fact, could look at a piece of lumber, smell it, and tell you all about the tree it came from. Dad borrowed $500 from my grandfather in 1948, and used salvaged materials from a demolished Minneapolis school building, to construct the house I grew up in. He repaid the loan in two years, so there was never a house payment, a good thing because Dad suffered from asthma, emphysema, and finally cancer. He spent much of his life in and out of hospitals.

The story doesn't end there. Mom and Dad had wanted to move into another house he was building at the time, the *Oakwood house*, totally nestled in the woods just north of Minneapolis. But right after the war, it was still hard to get building materials. It generally took 10 feet of well-pipe to reach good water in Bloomington, but the *Oakwood house* required 100 feet. Ten would have been possible, but not 100, and we needed a home, so we moved to the house I grew up in and the *Oakwood house* was sold later. Many years afterward, I learned that, had we grown up in the nicer home, we would have been drinking extremely toxic water, polluted by an abandoned munitions plant nearby. An attorney fought the Pentagon for years, and finally, about 2014, got some settlement for the people who either died or were made extremely sick from that water. My family was spared by 10 feet of pipe.

The last time I saw Dad alive in his garage, where he kept all his tools and did all his own car repairs, I found him fiddling with the leads from a worn-out headlight and car battery.

"See," he explained. "High beam never wears out. The battery won't run the car anymore, but if you touch the headlight to the posts the right way, high beams light up. Keep 'em in a box in the trunk and you've got an emergency light, in case you break down on the highway." Then he insisted on going one last time to the attic of the garage, the place where he kept building materials and anything that might be useful later. I literally carried him up the stairs. When we arrived at the top and turned on the light, Dad sat on a small saw horse. "Never buy nails," he proclaimed as his arm swept weakly over dozens of partially filled boxes and kegs of every size nail known to the civilized world.

After Dad got too sick to maintain his own small business, someone he built a home for got him a job in the carpenter shop at the University of Minnesota. He had only a high school education, but ended up as a supervisory engineer because he could walk into a building and tell you what structural deficiencies were present. He could tell you what needed to be looked at in 3 years, and what should be addressed immediately so the roof wouldn't collapse.

"They wouldn't let me do it today," his boss told me after dad died in 1981. "I put him in that position because he was better than any of the degreed engineers we could find."

I wish my Dad could have ended up in the Pentagon. He wasn't ready to be a peace activist, but he wouldn't have allowed our massive military operations to use the planet as a toxic dumping ground.

SEVENTEEN

Dad's older brother Vernon told me once he felt guilty. "Your dad was smarter than me. He should have been the one to go to college, but they sent me because I was going to be a minister." Uncle Vernon walked with an iron brace on one leg, and we grew up only with the story he'd been shot in the war. When Dad died, and I began spending more time with Uncle Vernon, I asked him, "What happened to your leg?" His story went like this:

> When your dad and I were boys, our dad had a worker who was so strong he could hold a construction wheelbarrow straight out, one-handed, but he was weakened by deep depression. "Ted," he'd say, "I can do any work you give me, even dig a basement myself if the horses are tired, but I need your jokes and stories when I get down."
>
> When I grew up and was wounded in World War Two, some German farmers saved me with a wheelbarrow. I was a warrant officer in Omar Bradley's Army. I was rushing back from headquarters to catch up with our unit after delivering a dead soldier's body, and money some of the men wanted sent home to family. I thought we were in a safe zone, but suddenly I saw a sniper lying in the ditch. I yelled to my driver to step on it. The driver panicked and jumped from

the jeep. I was shot and ended up lying in the ditch myself.

When I regained consciousness, I found myself being moved in a wheelbarrow by some German farmers, part of the resistance, who carried me up to a place where they could safely wait for an Army ambulance to drive by. I'll always remember, it was Sunday, April 8, 1945, because I used to say, "That's what I get for working on Sunday."

I spent the next two years in and out of Army hospitals. Your dad hitchhiked down to see me in Texas, on his way home from the Berkeley job. It was hard, but the worst was how they took it at home. My mother was devastated. My dad, unlike his usual joking self, was just quiet, and I never really knew how he felt. I'm forever grateful, though, to God and those brave farmers, for sparing me and letting me live my life with my family and ministry.

My aunt and uncle are buried in Lakewood Cemetery in Minneapolis, not far from the enormous boulder celebrating the life and service of Paul and Sheila Wellstone. I don't remember ever hearing about it growing up, but my uncle's gravestone shows him to be the recipient of a Purple Heart.

EIGHTEEN

In 2013, the last of my five years as President of Veterans for Peace, my friend Steve McKeown led us in organizing a major August 27 event at the Frank Kellogg House in St. Paul. On August 27, 1928, in Paris, France, the Kellogg-Briand Pact was signed, making war illegal as a means of settling international differences. Interestingly, virtually no one, including our most progressive politicians, had ever heard of this. It was almost unknown that Republican, Frank Kellogg, then Secretary of State under President Coolidge, is the only Minnesotan to ever receive the Nobel Peace Prize for engineering this international treaty together with Aristide Briand of France. Most assumed that Kellogg Boulevard, running by our State Capitol, had some affiliation with cereals that go snap, crackle, and pop.

Steve McKeown, Vietnam veteran and visionary co-founder of our group, remembered hearing about this in high school, and sometime around 2009 gave me a copy of "To End War: The Story of the National Council for Prevention of War (1921-1946)", written by Frederick Libby in 1969.

In 2011, author David Swanson wrote "When the World Outlawed War", and encouraged our group to visit the Kellogg House, which is on the National Register of Public Places, but privately owned and not open to the public. Surprisingly, the residents were more than amenable and decided to help us tell the story.

After World War One, people around the world were so devastated they felt, almost in unison, that, "We must do everything we can to not let war like this happen again."

It was a time when the President would speak at Arlington on ***Decoration Day*** – which would become

Memorial Day in 1969 – saying, "We are gathered here to honor those who have given their lives for the country. The greatest tribute we can pay them is to work with every strength we have to prevent future wars." It was a time when Sal Levinson, a Chicago business attorney with no interest in matters of war and peace, discovered that most small businesses he worked with were severely harmed during World War One. To help business, Levinson started what came to be called the *Outlawry Movement.* This was enthusiastically pushed forward by a worldwide mobilization of organizations like Women's International League of Peace and Freedom, the Fellowship of Reconciliation, the Friends, and hundreds of other peace organizations no longer around. The result was the Kellogg-Briand Pact to outlaw war.

This was also a time of serious hearings in Congress to create legislation to make it impossible to profit financially from war after learning that some huge corporations increased profits as much as eight hundred percent from selling World War One armaments. Then, almost in a blur, those major corporations moved in and squashed the legislation. At the same time, many of them, from the U.S. and other Allied countries, secretly sold arms that helped the early military buildup of Nazi Germany.

After this, if the Kellogg-Briand Pact was mentioned at all, it was dismissed as naïve and impractical because it didn't end war. The agreement was not given any enforcement power, though it's also never been rescinded. It's still listed on the U.S. Secretary of State website, with more than eighty cosignatory nations.

The law against driving drunk hasn't totally stopped people from committing that illegal act, but thankfully it's there, and we often save lives by enforcing it. Our event at the house suggested the Kellogg-Briand Pact should be better known and enforced.

NINETEEN

People who should know better spend large amounts of money doing studies to figure out why too many children aren't physically fit, or are getting diseases like diabetes, formerly associated just with older folks. When we were growing up, partly before TV, and certainly before proliferation of channels and advertising to pay for programs, the answer to the question, "What can I do?" was, "Go outside and play."

Children longed then, like today, for occasional treats, a candy bar or can of pop, but my mother was a nurse. She read *Prevention* magazine back in the 50s, and we were trained to think it a treat to get our own little Morton salt shaker to use on a tomato or a hardboiled egg as we walked around the backyard. We didn't know then about too much salt, but I think we could tell how much tasted good, and that wasn't too much. Too much of anything is generally not good, and I think the too much salt issue emerged largely thru advertising fast food as regular meal. I know they've been working to be healthier, but fast food has generally been something akin to a candy bar playing the part of a meal.

TV advertising is expensive. The Super Bowl has always been the costliest because it usually reaches the largest number of viewers. This includes children viewing ads glamorizing longed for, "occasional treats" as daily necessities. When I was a school specialist, teaching storytelling and video, I recorded the super bowl ads and picked a few that were fun and ok to show to children. When we looked at the ads and discussed the video tricks used to make them, we also talked about the dollar cost. Back then, it was only about a million dollars to buy a 30 second ad slot. This was also a time when one could buy a pretty good house for a family for $100,000. So we talked about things like that, things people need but don't always have. Then I asked them to work with the question, "Ok, suppose you have a million dollars to buy 30 seconds and maybe another million to produce the message to tell people to buy this kind of pop. Suppose you think there are better ways to use the money. What would you do?"

Some of the reports were pretty self-indulgent, but there were also great glimmerings of early social consciousness, from making healthy food available to everyone, to dealing with the social devastation some believe is caused by too much money spent worldwide on warfare, as in the famous Eisenhower quote about bombs and missiles stealing food and housing from people in need.

7. Having your cake and being too tired to eat it.

TWENTY

There is an old free speech standard, that one's speech should be limited only by actions comparable to falsely shouting fire in a crowded theatre. We have fire drills in school so children can practice exiting in calm, orderly fashion in the event of the panic of fire.

Occasionally there's a news piece about people being killed by a disorderly stampede in a sports stadium, and clearly the *Do not cry* ***fire!*** dictum was made to limit false speech that might cause this type of harm or death.

Free speech and the threat of censorship have always been problematic, but moving much of our entertainment or political theater to electronic media has greatly amplified the issue. In the early 80s, when I was immersed in the world of children's media, I was horrified to hear one of my closest friends tell the story of his first wife. Walking in Boston at night, she was attacked by a group who set her on fire. The thought, "I've heard this story before," haunted me. When I checked into it, I realized that one of the prime anecdotal arguments against excessive media violence was the story of a movie where teenagers used gasoline to set fire to a drunk on the beach, a movie the attackers in Boston had watched the night before setting my friend's wife on fire. If anyone tries to curb violence by banning similar media portrayals, there is an immediate cry of "Censorship! Normal people don't imitate such violence. Only people who are already deranged `do such things."

I do not intend to give you a comprehensive argument, just my story. George Gerbner, media violence researcher for the surgeon general, often said, "Bad things happen, and we need them in the stories, so we can show good ways of resolving the problems that are in our world." He also said that surveys generally show people do not support the proliferation of graphic violence from producers who defend the practice with: "We're just giving people what they want." Gerbner's analysis suggested that many producers make violent programs with the intent of easy sale internationally, thus increasing market share. Graphic sex and violence are much less expensive to translate into other languages than are more complex narratives, leading to the somewhat disingenuous claim, "This is what the audience wants." I pay attention when a film graphically portrays some horrendous act, and another equally powerful movie develops the disaster through the story line, with visuals focused on dramatic resolution to the problem. If the visual is grotesque violence, that's where the power is. If it shows solution to a problem, even violence, that's the power more likely to be imitated.

It is now possible to buy video games based on brutal battlefield experience, where players can kill American soldiers. I know of at least one situation where a mother, justifiably enraged, tried to stop sales of such games because she had just lost her son in Iraq. She was immediately stomped by the censorship lobby, including teenage expert witnesses, who argued, "It's not right for you to take away our fun."

Some people get officially labeled mentally ill. I believe we all have our levels of being ***off***, and I'm going to exercise my free speech privilege to say there may be no official label for it, but I believe that viewing war or any kind of killing as fun, is exceptionally deranged.

TWENTY-ONE

Growing up, most of the talk I heard about war was either John Wayne media-hype, or religious rhetoric in the vein of, "Kill a Communist for God." Only one adult, my Grandpa Meline, talked to us straight out, honestly, about war. Grandpa Meline, my mom's dad, was the fun grandfather. He's the one who took us fishing and had a basement full of amazing artifacts like old car licenses, the glider my uncle built at age 15, an old Victrola record player, and more. His basement was a museum. He's the one who mounted a pole in the yard and said, "Boys, there are silver dollars on top of the pole. When you learn how to climb to the top, you can have them."

8. Ceremony at the Lindstrom Veterans Memorial, Barry Riesch, Veterans for Peace, ringing a bell to call for less war, therefore fewer veterans and an end to equivocating about veterans' care.

We did, my brother and I; we became the best climbers in town.

One day, Grandpa Meline took my brother and I uptown as he took his turn raising the flag for both the town and for the veterans group he belonged to. He showed us how and why to respect the flag, how to fold it properly, not letting it touch the ground. On this day, he was much more serious than usual, but we were listening. In the middle of the flag ceremony, he just broke.

"Boys," he said, "war is a horrible thing. I was in World War One, and my brother died there. I hope neither of you ever have to go." My own brother, later diagnosed with a mental illness, automatically received a draft deferment. I had to go, though the assignment I got was pretty benign, maybe due to my grandfather's blessing. I pray we can move toward a time when that blessing expands, and no one has to go to war.

TWENTY-TWO

Most of the time I worked in schools, I specialized in teaching storytelling and video, health and environment. Same as a music or physical education teacher, I saw all the grades in the school once a week. One time, a second grade class didn't show up on time, so after 10 minutes I went to see what was going on. I caught the end of a presentation by a special guest, a policeman and father of a girl in the class. He was a good storyteller, and it was obvious the children liked him. I listened to the end of his talk, then led the class to my room to use the time remaining.

I thought nothing more about it until the next year when the classroom teacher told me the dad/policeman had called and offered to come and talk again. Then she told me the amazing story he had when he called.

> The summer after I spoke to your class, I was called to a shooting on the north side. A large crowd had gathered, the situation tense. The shooter saw my uniform, turned and pointed his gun at me. Just as I feared the worst, a little boy – I later learned he was a student in your class – looked at the shooter, then at me and shouted, "Don't shoot him. That's Eva's Dad."
>
> The boy's plea so disoriented the man, the other officers on the scene were able to get the gun away and arrest him. I feel like the talk I gave to your class probably saved my life. I'd be glad to do more of it.

So you may never know the powerful force of being who you are; the power of telling stories to children.

TWENTY-THREE

At one time, my wife Elaine and I had our names inscribed on the wall at *Amway* headquarters in Michigan in recognition for building our *Amway* sales to the first magic level, ***Platinum***. A friend had recommended this business opportunity at a time I was fighting to regain my health after working in a school full of mold. I was also fighting at the time to get the mold-infested school building remediated in a system where some teachers, also very ill, wouldn't go to a remediation strategy meeting, even off-site, for fear the administration would find out. In the midst of this, I was swayed, perhaps unwisely, by an *Amway* leader telling me their system would let me build an independent income, freeing me, he said, "to do anything you want with education."

This was 1996, and *Amway* was going to internet delivery, which seemed a better shopping system than cars driving everywhere. I was impressed that Frank Feather, who often uses the phrase, "Think globally, act locally," wrote a book about the *Amway* system, which began in 1959. I was particularly interested in *Amway's* strong environmental and health products, but especially intrigued that the environmental focus was coming from a company with the same heavy Republican overtones I'd grown up with. For years, I leaned more-and-more Democrat, but *Amway* struck my fascination with the potential for people with different ideas to work together for the good of all.

Nutrilite, the oldest organic vitamin company in the world, is owned by Amway. Getting on a *Nutrilite* regimen, as well as use of the excellent Amway air treatment system, was a big factor in restoring my health after being damaged by a bad school building. But a problem arose at our first big training to become *Amway* representatives. A former Congressman turned *Amway* distributor, addressed our group, railing against everything Elaine and I believed. We walked out, disgusted, thinking, "We signed on to build an independent business, not to be told how to think."

Our leaders told us to report this to the Corporation, because *Amway* had a Right to Differ policy that said trainers had no right to advocate religious or political philosophies that might turn off those who believe differently. The Corporation thanked us, and said they'd stop it, but they never did. This kind of thing happened frequently, and we regularly lost team members with less tolerance for the big picture than we had.

After the U.S. invaded Iraq in 2003, we attended a training where the speaker asked veterans to stand. I feared I was going to be used to honor what I believed to be an illegal war, but I stood up anyway. As I did, fighter jets flashed on the screen, accompanied by people cheering wildly. My right hand went high with a peace sign. I was angry. Elaine encouraged me to talk to the head of the training organization, who could not understand my difficulty with what was done. I knew in that moment we had already dropped out.

I had spent most of my life as a peace activist thinking, "You're not really a veteran. You never did anything dangerous." I went home from the *Amway* training and filled out the Veterans for Peace membership form, which had long languished on my desk. Suddenly I was an official veteran, one who was once asked to swear to protect the Constitution from all enemies, foreign and domestic.

War and Peace have nothing to do with Party affiliation. Secretary of Defense McNamara, Democrat in both the Kennedy and Johnson Administrations, years after the War in Vietnam ended, said, "I'm sorry. We knew at the time we had no business being there."

Republican President George W. Bush claimed that we were invading Iraq because Saddam Hussein has weapons of mass destruction. It makes no difference. Those who use falsehoods to put young people in dangerous, life-threatening situations, are enemies of the Constitution, enemies of the people.

TWENTY-FOUR

The difficulty of being a medic in Germany in 1971 was that we mostly had nothing to do. We were supposed to stand around acting like we were busy, and of course, we had to be ready when we were really needed. I managed to get myself on night duty, where I could sit at the desk and read, deal with occasional emergencies myself, or call a doctor if necessary. I learned to understand when the doctor, a draftee like me, was essential, and when he was not. Doctors were totally willing to do what was needed, but not wild about being called in the middle of the night to tell a new mom that her baby's temperature was not too high.

The training and experience served me well when I got back home. I ran camps a few more years, and also served as the camp nurse we otherwise had no budget for. My last few years working in schools, Iraq War driven budget cuts were rampant. Several times I walked into the office for some reason or another, only to find workers distraught

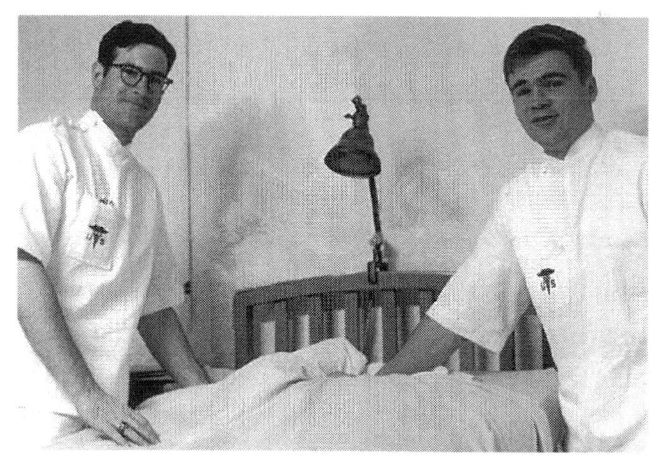

9. Army medics safe in Germany.

because they had a sick student but no nurse available in the immediate system. My medic training kicked in. I knew what to do. But how many times was this happening around the country where no one understood the problem?

I clipped out a news article at the time about Pentagon spending cuts devastating to a southern Minnesota candy company that would be forced to lay off workers. Obviously this involved contracts with PX stores on military bases around the world. Having a job is truly important, but wouldn't it be great if we could move people getting paid to do nothing, into positions where they could feel good about helping a lot of people? I think I'll paraphrase the old slogan, "I dreamed the Pentagon had to raise funds with candy sales, and schools had all the money they needed for teachers to teach, and to fund nurses to make sure students are well enough to learn."

TWENTY-FIVE

I've heard people shouting loudly, "No wonder the world is a mess. They won't even let us hang the Ten Commandments on the wall in school." And when I hear that, I calmly respond, "I don't understand. As a specialist, I didn't always have my own room, but when I did, I always hung the Ten Commandments up on the wall."

Some folks are more interested in shouting than listening, but occasionally someone asks, "What do you mean? How can you do that?"

I reply, "I have a beautiful poster with the Golden Rule, as stated in about 15 different spiritual traditions. Christianity, of course, goes like this: In everything, do to others as you would have them do to you. Buddhism says: Treat not others in ways that you yourself would find hurtful. Hinduism states: This is the sum of duty: do not do to others what would cause pain if done to you."

The usual reaction is, "The Golden Rule is not the Ten Commandments."

"Yes, it is," I say. "Look at Matthew 22". This is one of the places where the religious leaders tried to set Jesus up, to get him to say something they might use against him. The question they ask Jesus was, "Oh, great teacher, which of the Ten Commandments is most important?"

Jesus replied, "You can't single out one Commandment. They're all important and rolled up in one. Love God with all your heart and your neighbor as yourself."

If you argue that Buddhists and Hindus did not say, "Love God and your neighbor," I would point out that, in Matthew 25, Jesus said, "If you treat other people badly, you're treating me badly, and I am God." I know some people don't believe that Jesus is God, but people who shout about the Bible do, so my Golden Rule poster is the Ten Commands hanging on the wall. The difficulty is that most of this kind of thinking and screaming is run neither by love nor by logic.

TWENTY-SIX

My grandparents taught me to love gardening. And my Grandpa loved baseball and the fact that I played. I've always had a garden, and once I thought I'd write a story called *Vegetables in the Outfield* about a right fielder who tended a small garden because the ball rarely made it to the outfield.

In grade school, I played Little League ball. We walked regularly past the neighbor's garden behind our house to where Wayne Terwilliger lived. "The Twig" played second base for the minor league Minneapolis Millers 1955-57, and years later he surfaced as the highly respected coach who helped the Minnesota Twins win the World Series in 1987 and 1991. We mowed his lawn and were paid with used baseballs, and cracked bats, which he showed us how to fix. He showed us how to make double plays, and when our team came from a slow start and ended up in the Bloomington BAA championship, the Twig came to our final game at Legion Field. We won.

One baseball tip the Twig taught us was something I have since taught to many children, as a life lesson. He said, "A lot of time in baseball, it seems you're just standing there with nothing to do. That's the problem. What if the ball comes to you, and you panic? When the pitcher is winding up, pay attention to where the runners are. Think, if the ball comes to me, where should I be throwing it. If you've thought about it ahead of time, you can calmly do the right thing."

I called the Twig after seeing him on TV in the World Series. He came to my school to talk baseball and life lessons. The kids loved him, and he later wrote back and included a poem he'd made with all their names.

10. Wayne Terwilliger, the "Twig", a great ballplayer, even greater coach and an outstanding person.

Fifteen years later, after my grandson Tyler and I had finished that 61-mile hike, the St. Paul Saints minor league team invited us to throw out the first pitch and lead singing at seventh inning stretch. The Twig actually coached the Saints for a while, after giving up his Twins job. When the Saints' PR person asked, "Anything else you'd like, besides throwing the first pitch and song?" I answered, without having thought about it, "Yes, any way you could get Wayne Terwilliger back for the night?" The PR man smiled and said, "You're in luck. He's coaching the Fort Worth Cats now, and that's who we're playing." When we walked across the field so Tyler could throw out the first ball, I continued to the Cats' dugout to say hello. The Twig looked up and said, "Why do I know you?" I told him, "You helped us win the Little League championship in Bloomington, and you write great poetry for school kids you talk to." The Twig reached out, grinned, and shook my hand.

TWENTY-SEVEN

It's been a long time since I believed it, but I grew up in a system where things like cleaning and cooking were considered women's work. I tried in vain to get my mom to teach me to cook, but finally got her to teach me to make poached eggs. She consented, maybe only because that's what they fed us the morning of district wrestling tournaments.

The military, I think, is still the epitome of a ***macho*** system, but long before women were allowed in as soldiers, cleaning was central to the teaching of discipline.

My friend John and I won third place in the Fort Sam Houston talent contest. A very good G.I. rock band wiped us out and took first, but we were the only ones to get a standing ovation, I think because we pushed the system as far as you could without getting into real trouble. I used the melody of *O Christmas Tree* to write a song called *Oh Army Green*, and John, a guitar player and musician, set it to a more-hip rock tune to give it more class when we sang:

> Oh Army Green, Our Army Green. We wear it to mop our latrine.
>
> Our uniforms are all the same, and no one calls us by our name,
>
> But when we wear our army green, you'll know that our latrine is clean.

Cleaning keeps people healthy, but when it's imposed by ruthless dictators who have forgotten that, or simply don't know, it's just annoying. A few years ago, we were cleaning up after a veterans' holiday party, and one of the older women said, "Boy, you vets really know how to clean."

I responded, "Well, of course. Don't you know? It was a central part of the training, but I suppose they're outsourcing it now."

Immediately, someone said, "They are."

Well, if they are, I hope they're not paying private contractors three times a soldier's wage to do it, unless it's women who still generally get less than their male counterparts. I would also ask, if it was so crucial to learning discipline back then, what's changed?

TWENTY-EIGHT

In 1996, I attended *Stand for Children*, a massive gathering organized by Children's Defense Fund in Washington D.C. I had always wanted to go to the Vietnam Wall, but by the time the daylong rally ended, it was late afternoon. The place to get a map for finding names was closed, so I decided I would read the entire wall to find the names I was looking for. Several hours later, as it was getting too dark to see, I had to acknowledge that reading the entire Wall was an unwieldy task. Thinking I should come back another time to use the guide, I read one more section and saw something I wasn't counting on. There was my name, including middle initial, LARRY D. JOHNSON.

Before the advent of cell phones, there were 100 Larry Johnson listings in the Minneapolis phone book, but only four Larry D. Johnson. My mother had died 5 years earlier, but I could hear her clearly, saying, "Use your middle initial so you don't get mixed up with other people." I felt like I was hovering above the Wall in trance, or maybe as a spirit. I was grateful to be alive, penetrated at the same time with the reality of how easily my exact name on that wall could have been me.

Almost thirty years after the end of the war in Vietnam, Robert McNamara, Secretary of Defense from 1961 to 1968, publicly said something like, Well, gee, uh, well, we knew at the time we shouldn't be there. Well, gee, uh, well, uh, gee, I'm sorry. He lived out a relatively long life, taking advantage of lucrative jobs and other offers that come from high-level government service. On that Wall are the names of too many young people who never even got to live their lives.

On another wall nearby, the Franklin D. Roosevelt Memorial, there is a striking quote from 1943, two years before the end of World War Two: "Unless the peace that follows recognizes that the whole world is one neighborhood and does justice to the whole human race, the germs of another world war will remain as a constant threat to mankind."

TWENTY-NINE

Somebody said once, "The first casualty of war is the ***Truth***."

And whenever the latest scandal comes out, whether military sexual assault, blatant killing of civilians, grotesque torture, or lack of oversight at nuclear facilities, the response is something like, "That's just a few bad people. We'll fix it."

When more of the ***Truth*** comes out, it's, "We had no idea, but we're working to correct it. We can't make too much of this, or it will hurt morale and the mission."

The problem is that all of this is untrue. I will admit that my bias is searching for high level, nonviolent means of resolving international conflict, but for an operation that parades around in cloaks of honor, loyalty, and often the trappings of Christianity itself, I'd prefer stronger adherence to ***Truth***. When people, meaning to be respectful, say, "Thank you for fighting for our freedom," I'd prefer they paraphrase Jesus and say, "Thank you for fighting for the ***Truth*** so it can set us free."

Those of us who entered the Army as conscientious objectors had all the same training as everyone else, except for using weapons. The closest we got to weapons was the night we all crawled under what the drill sergeant said was live ammunition. By the time this happened, I felt like I could count on nothing except to possibly stay out of trouble if I did everything they said. As I low-crawled across a field lit only by explosions above, my only thought was, "Live ammunition. Right. I should stand up and prove they're lying about this too."

Being Scandinavian, mellow and always relatively low key, I believed I was totally under control; but I was so angry, so close to standing up, it's horrifying to think back to that night. Thirty years later, I finally told this story in a men's retreat where we were trying to sort out our varied experiences in the 60s. A friend, the only other person in the group who was in the military, told me, "It was live ammunition. Someone in our unit did stand up, and he was killed."

It doesn't matter whether he stood up out of panic or due to some presumed, rational, social science experiment like I was contemplating. He stood up, and his life ended, though I would guess his death was reported as some kind of sacrifice so we could all have freedom.

THIRTY

They called it *Agent Orange*, like the main character in a spy novel, or a talking pumpkin in a scary children's cartoon. They said it wouldn't hurt you. They sprayed it on the jungles in Vietnam to kill all the hiding places so the bad guys couldn't kill you.

Fifty years later, we know the agent is still killing civilians over there and veterans over here, while the companies who made it are killing all attempts to hold them responsible for creating the carcinogenic defoliant called Agent Orange. They're too busy making milder versions to spray on the lawn, accompanied by signs that imply that won't hurt you either. "Just don't let children or pets walk on the lawn for two days."

In 1942, E.J. Kraus, a botanist at the University of Chicago, discovered a chemical means of killing vegetation and turned it over to the military, thinking something about the herbicide might be valuable.

In 1943, the biologist Arthur Galston did his Ph.D. dissertation on a means to make soybeans grow faster. He also discovered, independently of Kraus, that higher concentrations would defoliate and kill the soybeans. In 1951, unknown to Galston, biological warfare scientists, using the Kraus research, began producing Agent Orange, which would later be used to kill jungle vegetation and expose enemy hiding places during the Vietnam War. In 1965, while teaching at Yale, Galston began lobbying both his scientific colleagues and the U.S. government to stop using Agent Orange, because of the horrendous impact it had on Vietnamese civilians and American soldiers. Some 20 million gallons of the toxic chemical were dumped on Vietnam between 1962 and 1972. By the time it was banned, it was much too late for the people of Vietnam and too many American veterans. Many vets are still fighting for their health and for justice around the issue of Agent Orange exposure.

A few years ago, I went to my city council and said, "I don't use chemicals on my lawn and garden. If the neighbors are using them, it shouldn't be allowed that it float onto my yard. Besides, most of that stuff is made by the same companies that gave us chemicals like Agent Orange, and I don't believe in supporting companies that don't support the troops."

A row of stunned faces stared back at me. Then, a council member related to a Vietnam veteran said, "You're right, you know. I just never thought of it that way."

Well, OK, good, but we should have been thinking of it that way when we first let the manufacturers get away with telling soldiers, "Don't worry. Agent Orange won't hurt you." The same goes for all the more recent war toxins, like depleted uranium.

THIRTY-ONE

I've never understood folks who put their hands on their hips, screw their faces into a scowl and mutter, "They won't even let us pray in school."

I've always prayed in school. Teaching is hard, and one needs all the help they can get to help children become imaginative, productive citizens of the world. I've just never been interested in getting up front and imposing my way of praying on everybody else. In fact, it was Jesus in Matthew 6 who instructed us not to get up in front of everyone and show off when we pray. He said to find a secret place and just talk to God about what's needed.

Psalm 121, from the part of the book shared by Jews and Christians, says, "I will lift my eyes to the hills, where my help comes from. My help comes from God, who made everything."

11. Playing Beethoven's *Ode to Joy* on a *Bubble Trumpet*, made from items rescued from the landfill because they won't compost like leaves on the forest floor.

Being from Minnesota, and loving the giant Redwoods of California, I say it a little differently. "I lift my eyes to the tallest trees, to breathe-in my help."

Elaine always says I pray at the compost pile, and I've always taught children that trees are the ultimate example of composting; or, if you will, of life, death, and resurrection. The leaves fall, along with old trees, to decompose and become vibrant forest floor soil to keep trees growing. Then as the trees breathe in the air and collect the carbon dioxide, which they want, they give out the oxygen which we want. We breathe in the oxygen, and our heart pumps the blood past the lungs to collect it and take that oxygen all through our bodies to keep us dynamically alive.

There's an old Christian hymn, *Breathe on Me, Breath of God*, and I believe I'm praying whenever I thankfully inhale that breath of God and let it flow thru my body to give it the life to strive to love all my neighbors as myself.

I am aware that too often those who complain, "They won't let us pray in school," do not complain about letting horrendous toxins get into the holy air they breathe. In fact, too often they encourage and foster it with forms of deregulation.

Paul, in First Corinthians, says our bodies are temples of the Holy Spirit. We now know considerably more about how bad air – fouling the breath of God – makes people physically, and sometimes emotionally, sick to the point where they harm themselves and others. I'd say "Pray without ceasing," in your own way, quietly, in school and everywhere there's clean air.

Ask God for clean air, and demand it from those who claim to be his or her representatives on Earth.

THIRTY-TWO

The emotion of standing on the field at graduation from medic training in late February 1971 is lodged in my body. My closest Army friend, John, wanted the same assignment as I did. We both conscientiously opposed taking of another's life. We had helped each other through the training itself, and through our weekend-pass trips to the folk music clubs in San Antonio. We were truly ready for anything, but we hoped we would not be going to Nam.

After the congratulatory statements about making it through this important training, they said, "Half of you are going to Korea. You'll be there for the remainder of your duty. The rest of you are going to Germany. You'll be there 3 months before shipping out to Nam." John's name came up: Korea. Then mine: Germany. I was going to Vietnam. My friend was not.

After working in the clinic in Germany about 3 months, I got a package with a letter and a boomerang. John was in Australia, on R & R, enjoying a brief escape from the early part of his tour of duty in Vietnam before heading back to the jungle to complete the tour. The news came as no surprise. We couldn't count on anything we were told, but I still feel extremely fortunate. They regularly implied we would be sent to Vietnam. I stayed in Germany until my discharge in 1972.

I did try several times to find my friend after we returned to civilian life, but mine got intense; just trying to find work and a way back into the *world*. John and I both came from Minneapolis, though we didn't know each other before basic training. I tried calling everyone I could find with John's last name. No one knew him, or my worst fear, something had happened, and they didn't want to talk about it. After my 61-mile hike in 2007, I tried once again to find John, this time using a new tool, the Internet. As it turned out, John's medic training inspired him to become a doctor. He lived out west. He had tried a number of times to find me, but wading through all the Larry Johnson's in the Minneapolis phone book was like being back in the jungle.

When we did finally reconnect, we spent two hours on the phone. Despite the passage of 35 years – both of us were over 60 – we picked up exactly where we had left off back in Texas training. Two things John said struck me intensely.

"The first time we faced enemy fire, I was scared. All I had was my medic bag. Then suddenly, all the guys in my unit were standing in a circle around me, weapons in the air. I realized they knew that if something happened to me, there was no one to take care of them. I realized I was the most protected man in the unit. God is good."

The other thing he told me was, "There was one other medic, in our unit, who I got about as close to as you and I were. One time, he asked to trade duty with me. The commanding officer okayed it, and he went out on a mission I was supposed to be on. He did not return alive."

I'm sorry for the other medic, and for his family. But I'm glad my friend came back. I know he's making an enormous contribution to the lives of many.

THIRTY-THREE

The 61-mile hike was designed to raise money for two projects, the first to help end or significantly reduce war, the other, a live streaming video project to allow soldiers in Iraq to easily visit with family back home. There was some money raised, but nothing like I had planned. The only infrastructure we had to accomplish this was a loaned-website designed to collect donations. We counted on the promises of much media coverage to direct people to that site.

Almost all of that promise evaporated when the 35W bridge over the Mississippi collapsed one week before the hike. For weeks after the hike, the entire world was treated to the tragedy of the many cars, and school bus from a settlement house, that fell into the river when the big bridge went down. Much time and money was spent discussing how such a tragedy could happen and who to blame. There were no evident answers, just high viewership without the need for costly pre-produced programming.

Part of my preparation for media coverage was to provide a fairly accurate timeline of where we'd be and when. The first day of the hike, a friend, Andy Mickel, caught up with us half way to Lindstrom on his weekly bike ride. Andy gave me a 1961 half-dollar, explaining it was one of those magic numbers that read the same upside down. It happened in 1881, 1961, and wouldn't happen again till 6009. Later, I looked into it and found these described as strobogrammatic numbers, interesting to numerologists, but not to professional mathematicians. I'm not either one, but I love stories connected to numbers, and a lot of numbers-magic came up.

12. In 1961, I walked around the block on homemade stilts to prepare for the 50-mile hike. In 2016, at Fort Snelling, I found I could at least still walk on stilts.

In 1961 the Soviets detonated the largest thermonuclear test explosion up to that time. They weren't first to test H-Bombs, so later that year they made Yuri Gagarin, the first human in space.

We never heard of such things at the time, but Frederick McKinley Jones died in 1961. He was the African-American, World War I Veteran, mechanical inventor genius whose patents helped launch *Thermo King*.

1961 was the year President Kennedy sent 400 advisors and helicopters to Saigon, an event some say, when taking partisan sides, is how Kennedy got us into the War in Vietnam. Usually ignored is that about a month before his assassination, Kennedy signed an executive order to remove all personnel from Vietnam by 1965 (strategically scheduled for after the election in 1964). Kennedy's order to pull troops out of the conflict was rescinded almost immediately after he was killed.

In 1961, the Henry Mancini & Johnny Mercer song *Moon River* was made famous in the movie, *Breakfast at Tiffany's.* Years later, *Moon River* was also featured in the film, *Born on the Fourth of July*, the true story of Ron Kovic, a disabled former Marine and an early leader in Vietnam Veterans Against the War.

Joseph Heller's book "Catch 22" also came out in 1961. The protagonist, Captain John Yossarian, a World War Two combat pilot, is trying to maintain his sanity by not flying endless combat missions. The hitch is the clause known as *Catch 22* – If you're crazy, you aren't fit to fly any more combat missions. All you have to do is ask. However, if you're sane enough to ask to get out of such insane danger, you're clearly sane enough to keep flying. Carry on.

THIRTY-FOUR

I wrote my conscientious objection statement in 1970 at a time when I was immersed in some of the many systems that believed we're the only ones who really believe the Bible to be literally true in the right way. I had been working in Minneapolis for Youth for Christ, the organization Billy Graham emerged from, and I'd already witnessed some doctrinal trouncing between different denominations supposedly united in bringing the entire world to Jesus.

I was a rising star, until I decided the literal truth of the Bible forbade killing, even in war, based on historical documentation of the early Christians. At that point I experienced severe judgment from former colleagues.

"You know," they screamed, "God had his hands in a lot of wars in the Old Testament" meaning I was absolutely wrong, and in some cases, bound for eternal damnation. But my Bible understanding was that the Old Testament teachings had been fulfilled and improved on in the New Testament, which put a greater emphasis on love. If one is to take the Old Testament God commanding his people to go to war ***then*** as reason to go to war ***now***, it would be important to be consistent. The Old Testament is strewn with requirements for the death penalty for infractions like sassing one's parents, taking the name of the Lord in vain, or for engaging in sexual relations outside of marriage. Following these commands would prevent wars, because there would be no one left to fight them, but it would also cut too many lives short, as war still does today.

If I were using an Old Testament passage to justify war, I'd choose the story of David and Goliath. Israel was fighting the Philistines who had a big guy, the 9-foot-tall Goliath.

"Let's settle this man to man," Goliath screamed. "Send your best warrior to fight me and whoever wins, wins for his side."

No one stepped up for the job, and about that time, David showed up to deliver lunch to his older soldier brothers. When David heard what was happening, he said, "If no one else will do it, I will. God will help me."

Goliath roared with laughter when gangly little David walked out with nothing but a slingshot. David's armor didn't fit and he was too small to hold a spear, but David had become expert with the slingshot. As a shepherd boy, he practiced for hours to while away the time sitting on the hillside watching the sheep. It was fun, but he was also serious about being good with the slingshot so he could stop predators from harming his flock. David calmly let go with one stone to kill the giant, and yes, somebody got killed, but it was just one person, not a pile of fighters on both sides. Of course, it's important to note that the Philistines honored their champion's commitment. In this moment, it probably doesn't matter if it was out of honor, or simply fear that the little shepherd boy had more stones and knew how to use them.

THIRTY-FIVE

It's been 60 years since we dropped nuclear bombs on two cities in Japan, and the argument rages on. Some say the bombs caused an early surrender and saved a lot of lives. Others say they were unnecessary because the Japanese were already prepared to surrender. Elaine had a wonderful high school history teacher, a veteran of World War Two, who believed in the need to drop the bomb, but encouraged diversity of thought, inspiring discussions. Elaine wrote a class paper arguing it was wrong to drop the bomb. The teacher graded her paper and commented, "I disagree with everything you've said, but you've written a wonderful paper and supported your arguments well. I'm giving you an A plus."

I consider that a model of excellent teaching, but rarely, if ever, does any discussion gravitate to the fact that those bombs, by their very nature, were a violation of international law because they killed scores of civilians. Both the Geneva Conventions and the Just War Theory say it's wrong to kill civilians. It's astounding to me that the oldest Christian church in Japan, one that survived years of persecution by non-Christian forces, was instantaneously vaporized by the Christian blessing on the atomic bomb unleashed on Nagasaki.

I hope Martin Luther doesn't mind, but I rewrote the words to *A Mighty Fortress is Our God.* I apologize, sort of, to the many Christians who don't believe in a literal Second Coming of Jesus, to the non-Christians who don't care, and the Hindus who wait for Krishna to come again. My experience is that those most adamant about the Second Coming of Christ are generally among the strongest supporters of grotesque arms build-up.

A mighty fortress is our Bomb, our ultimate creation.

God made the world in seven days, but we're the real sensation.

We'll blow it up in one, make dust clouds by the ton,

So thick they'll cloud the sun.

On earth there'll be no sequel.

When Christ the Lord returns to earth, in clouds with power from on high,

We'll think he's come from outer space, attacking us from in the sky.

Pray for delivery. Shoot your artillery,

That's what God wants to see.

Shoot down your Lord in the name of the Lord.

Amen.

THIRTY-SIX

One of the stories Elaine and I have told for many years is the *Legend of Sadako*, a young Hiroshima runner who folded more than 1,000 paper cranes to try to heal her "atom-bomb disease" and to bring peace to the world. In 2008, we were asked by Mayors for Peace to write a special letter to the Mayor of Hiroshima. Our telling of the story has always echoed the work of Mayors for Peace, an organization of several thousand mayors shouting worldwide, "It is never ok to bomb my city!"

Dear Mayor Akiba:

Elaine and I have told the story of Sadako and the Cranes many places in the U.S. and throughout the world since 1982. We have also taught many groups to fold the cranes and send them to Hiroshima through our friendship and association with Dr. Walter Enloe, former headmaster of Hiroshima International School.

We have heard the discussion about what to do with the enormous number of paper cranes sent to Hiroshima from children around the world. Though we're both strong environmental advocates, we support the effort to store and showcase these *treasures*, rather than burn or recycle them. We understand there would be expense to building a storage facility, but we believe the mass of collected cranes is a powerful embodiment of Sadako's prayer for her last folded crane to fly everywhere to tell people to never again drop such bombs as fell on Hiroshima and Nagasaki.

We live in a city where much promotion is done to persuade people to come to the Mall of America to shop. I know business activity is important to every city, but how much more noble to promote tourism to Hiroshima to see the Peace Park and cranes from around the world, genuinely pray for peace, and then do necessary business in the shops and hotels of Hiroshima.

THIRTY-SEVEN

REAL MEN may or may not eat quiche, but I believe they DO STAND UP TO RAPE, IN THE MILITARY AND AT HOME. When the first reports slid out about rampant military sexual assault, soldier-on-soldier, some of the reaction was, "That's not true. The rate of rape in the military is no higher than in civilian life," as if to suggest that therefore rape is not a problem.

The inevitable cover-up is probably no longer possible because too many brave women soldiers have spoken out about a situation that should have been stopped with high level prosecution the first time it happened. So how about all of us just stand against all violence and sexual assault, from playground bullying to military molestation. Rape, whether by officers or enlisted personnel, is a horrendous crime, as is rape of "enemy" during combat. It is all a despicable blot on all we say America stands for.

Civilian or military, we would all show the highest honor to take leadership in positive development of our own intimate relationships, and to work with other caregivers to help the children in our lives to grow up with healthy views of sexuality and relationships. I would ask the media to take responsibility in ending rampant use of sexuality as titillation, replacing it with gripping dramatizations of loving intimacy and sexual respect. What if churches, educational institutions, and indeed, the military, could ramp up deep discussions on the issue, asking, "How can we truly learn to love one another as neighbors, including, when appropriate, as intimate lovers?"

We love to argue about who is worse, or where things are worse, rather than just deciding what we can realistically do to let love, not violent lust, rule. All I can say is RAPE IS NEVER OK, ESPECIALLY IN THE MILITARY.

THIRTY-EIGHT

There's a verse in Romans 1:27 that often takes center stage in the God denounces homosexuality crusade. I have the Revised Standard Version Bible in front of me, and it reads, "men likewise gave up natural relations with women and were consumed with passion for one another, men committing shameless acts with men."

It seems pretty clear, until you read the verses on either side and see that God's Word is not just referring to sexual improprieties, but rather the entire outlay of human imperfection. This is not a Bible commentary, but given the way people quote the Book to justify whatever is their issue, I could easily make a case for this verse being against war. The passion men had for killing other men, as long as they were ***gooks***, horrified me in basic training. Personally, I believe men killing men, or women, is a shameless act, and that war separates men and women from natural relations with whomever the partner is they love. It's hard enough to develop solid love relationships, but war puts millions of people in a milieu of temptation toward prostitution, rape, and infidelity, certainly not acceptable to those who try to make Bible verses like these all about gay sex.

The Old Testament story of Sodom and Gomorrah, which also usually gets dragged into the condemnation, ends with Lot and his daughters holed up in a cave. The cities have been destroyed for gross unrighteousness, and Lot's wife has died as the family escaped.

Lot's daughters decide, "There's no one left for us to make babies with. Let's get our father drunk so he'll go along with getting us pregnant to perpetuate our family."

That's what they did, but any mention or discussion of this story rarely comes up in conservative Bible-pounding circles. Long after I was gone from the church I grew up in, the head of the denomination resigned quietly when his wife died of AIDS he inflicted on her. I don't know what had been going on in this man's life, but I do know that too many people living in a judgmental system feel they have to live a lie, even if their heart says no. I also know it was Jesus who said something like, "How can you see well enough to help your neighbor get the speck out of his eye, when you've got a logjam in your own?"

Incidentally, if you've got a speck, gently hold the eyelid up till your eye starts to water. The little irritant usually washes out. Medic? Yes, I was, but my mom was also a nurse.

THIRTY-NINE

I attended the University of Minnesota in the 60s. At the time, a group of us got credit for making anti-war radio documentaries. Father Bury, a campus Catholic priest aligned with the more famous Berrigan brothers, made anti-war statements we interspersed with quotes as in the famous speech by then Vice President Spiro Agnew, "The student now goes to college to proclaim, rather than to learn … A spirit of national masochism prevails, encouraged by an effete core of impudent snobs who characterize themselves as intellectuals."

Then we retreated to Annie's Parlour in Dinkytown to debrief. It was at Annie's Parlour that I announced I had done the kind of conscientious objection where, if drafted, I'd be a medic with no weapon. One of my co-producers blasted me, "You can't do that! You're just patching them up so they can kill some more." I hadn't thought this out, but my immediate reaction was, "No, I'm not. I'm patching them up so they can get back home where they belong."

Forty-five years after that experience, the Bookhouse, in Dinkytown, asked Elaine and I to facilitate a story gathering to remember and collect the early days of Dinkytown, particularly the 60s when activism was everywhere. The evening of storytelling alone was remarkable, but for me, even more wonderful, the Bookhouse paid us in books. I found a set of Edwin Way Teale's books: "North with the Spring", "Journey into Summer", "Autumn Across America" and "Wandering Through Winter".

Before getting drafted, I had loved the out of doors and ran camps. Then, while serving as a medic in Germany, I discovered that same set of Teale's books in the base library, and read it joyously. It's one of the things that kept me alive.

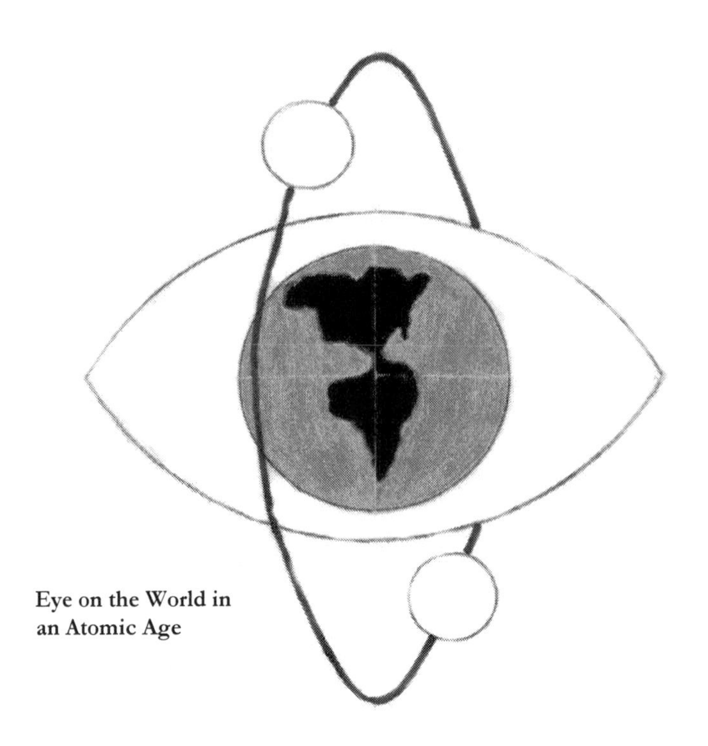

13. Logo made for a broadcast class in 1969 at the University of Minnesota.

I had signed on to be willing to save lives and get people back home, but I found myself working in a clinic where mostly we had nothing to do. We were supposed to look like we were busy, which meant that reading and writing were not legitimate. One of the doctors, drafted like us, had an enormous appliance box in his office. Medics besieged by meaningless regulations could go in his office and hide from the real Army, but that big box was too often occupied when I needed it.

Until I got myself assigned to undesirable night duty, where I worked alone, the doctor on call, I was seriously frustrated. That was when my friend Tucker stepped up. He first distinguished himself by suggesting, "Let's see how long we can grow our hair before anyone says anything." Tucker didn't mind standing around, bullshitting, ready to snap to attention as needed. He came to me and said, "Go read and write in the bathroom. Let me know where you are at all times, and in the unlikely event someone is looking for you specifically, I'll come and get you."

Reading, or writing, was not the work I was being paid practically nothing for, but I believe my contributions from that study have more than repaid the taxpayers. I only hope to someday find Tucker and publicly thank him. I don't know that my work back then got anyone home where they belonged, but I pray I am doing so now.

FORTY

I took my first wife to see the film M*A*S*H before I was drafted. I had already processed my conscientious objection, so I was interested in that war movie because I knew I'd be a medic if the draft board actually pulled my number. She was aghast, at the language and behavior, but once we were in Germany, and I was working at the clinic, she commented, "That movie was pretty accurate."

We were never interrupted by "incoming," but we needed a strong sense of humor to survive. It was a goofy place, though the doctors and most medics were serious about their work, on the rare occasion the work happened to be real. The doctors let some of us assist with minor surgery, not unlike what we would have done on our own serving in combat, but one guy, Price, was never allowed to do that. I don't know how he graduated as a medic, but he was in our unit, standing tall and ready to not care or listen to anything. One night in town, he knocked on my apartment door by mistake. German prejudice meant that the only places G.I.s with families could rent were buildings occupied by prostitutes, recent Turkish immigrants, or American soldiers. Our neighbor made her living providing comfort and relaxation privately to visitors from the military base, so as I got the baby back to sleep, Price went next door.

Medics gave a lot of penicillin shots, and I suppose Price could have cured himself, but maybe he was smart enough to not do that. Back at the clinic, his crowning achievement was the day he gave a smallpox vaccination to a one-month old child. It had been drilled into us, "Never give smallpox to a child younger than one years old. It could mean death."

Price did it anyway, but nothing happened, because he gave it wrong. I'm glad I was the only one giving shots to my own child, and I'm glad Price was confined to our benign German operation, and not out in combat where life and death happened all the time.

FORTY-ONE

There's a story in I Samuel 8 about Israel demanding a king so they could be like the other nations. Samuel, the current prophet, was distraught, believing God to be the King who protected them. When he checked in, God said, "Give them a king, if that's what they want, but please tell them the truth first. Tell them a king is going to take a lot of their money in taxes, and make people do a lot of things they'd rather not do, including sending them off to fight his wars."

And that's what happened. Later, when the boy-wonder David, slayer of Goliath, became king, he also taxed the people and sent out armies. In II Samuel 11, David sent the armies out to fight while he lounged on the roof of his palace, not unlike the way Tom Rix describes too many Vietnam leaders in his book, "The Generals".

From his palace roof, David saw a gorgeous woman, Bathsheba, bathing on the roof of one the lesser buildings in the kingdom. Though she was married to Uriah, one of David's soldiers, he invited her to spend the night. Feeling guilty, David called Uriah back, gave him special leave and said, "Go, make love to your wife." The next day, when David found Uriah sleeping on the steps of the palace, he asked, "What's wrong? I told you to be with your wife."

Uriah said, "Sir, thank you. I'm sorry. I can't do that when my comrades are still out there fighting and in danger." So, to honor such loyalty and commitment, King David sent Uriah back and ordered him be put in the thick of the fighting, where he was killed. Afterward, it was ok to marry Bathsheba, so he did, quickly, for the math to work out when the child was born.

A short time later, the prophet Nathan showed up and said, "David, I want to tell you a story." David liked stories, so Nathan told the king, "There was a rich man with one thousand sheep and a poor man with just one. The rich man had company coming. He didn't want to break up an even flock of sheep, so he sent his servant out to cook the poor man's sheep for dinner."

David was incensed by the rich man's behavior.

Then Nathan looked him in the eye and insisted, "David, you are the rich man in the story. It isn't enough that you have more than everybody else already? Now you have to take the life of one of your soldiers so you can have his wife? What is wrong with you?"

Bathsheba's child died shortly after birth, and David repented, praying forth the beautiful Psalm 51, "Create in me a clean heart, O God, and renew a right spirit within me." Uriah remained dead, as do too many soldiers, because too many rich guys want to sleep with their war profits. I heard a lot of Bible stories growing up. Nobody ever told me that one.

FORTY-TWO

After I was discharged, in the 70s, I maintained office space for my writing projects on whichever bus I'd chosen to ride. Frequently, I wrote short pieces on the OGP, the Old Gardening Party, for small, alternative journals, as well as for *Organic Gardening* magazine.

14. If you're running the OGP, I guess you gotta know how to grow corn.

We created OGP to keep the world safe for gardening, children, and storytelling. Originally called the Old Garbaging Party, our symbol was a dog tipping over garbage cans to make use of things that should have been composted. Wisdom later changed garbaging to gardening, replacing the dog and garbage can symbol with an earthworm aerating the soil by chewing dirt in one end and sending fertilizer castings out the other.

One night in 1979, I got a call from Tom Brazaitis, Washington Bureau Chief for the *Cleveland Plain Dealer.* He asked if I would consider a draft to run for President of the United States on the OGP ticket. It's not something I had even thought about, but it took only a moment to say, "I will not run, but I will proudly walk." Shortly after that, Brazaitis wrote the column nominating me, focusing mainly on the OGP tax position. The OGP believes no one should pay taxes at all until their income equals or exceeds that of the legislators deciding how tax money is spent. Those making less than legislators earn are required to fill out a lengthy form, giving ideas on cutting costs based on the vast experience of getting by on their current income. This forces the government to get money from those who have it, and solicits cost-cutting ideas from those who really understand.

Most people never even heard about it, and I did lose the Presidency to Ronald Reagan that year. However, occasionally over subsequent years, friends near Cleveland sent word that Tom Brazaitis was still plugging the OGP. On February 11, 2003, just before the U.S. invaded Iraq, he wrote a column, *War Protests Different Back in Era of the Draft*, that was distributed nationally. He wrote about Nixon resigning in disgrace, but remaining a hero to legions of young men because he ended the military draft.

Unlike the 60s, when virtually every young man faced the prospect of being sent off to war, Brazaitis reasoned that student concerns in the post-911 era are more theoretical. Draft age students are concerned about war the same way they're concerned about AIDS in Africa or poverty in America. It's a problem, but not one that affects them directly.

Brazaitis also quoted Representative Charlie Rangel: "Things today aren't much different from the Civil War, when men of means could hire substitutes to go fight and die for them. Only today, with the All-Volunteer Army, men of means don't even have to pull out their checkbooks. Their *Get Out of War Free Cards* are covered by taxes."

I kept the article, and when I did the 61-mile hike in 2007, I decided to talk with Tom Brazaitis again. That's when I learned, sadly, that he had died of cancer in 2005. I also learned he too had served two years in the Army in the 60s, in Germany, and, not surprisingly, that he was one of the few journalists speaking out in 2003 about the lies and corruption taking us into Iraq. I don't know who I respect less – journalists who were quiet or complicit in 2003, but talk tough on Iraq now, or those who still talk as if the mission accomplished in that effort was a success. Thanks, Tom, for calling me in 1979, and especially for the work you did for years after that. I'm sorry I never got to meet you in person.

FORTY-THREE

As leader of the OGP, I do things like play pretty good patriotic music on six feet of *swinging*, worn out garden hose. The message here is, "If the Pentagon can't figure out other ways to cut costs, maybe they could at least replace the large expense of military marching bands with individual brass players armed with worn out garden hose that would otherwise end up on the landfill."

Sometimes I do a show called Music for Weapons and Waste Reduction, playing an approximation of melody on Swing Hose, Heavy Metal Recycled Water Faucet, French Shoe Horn, and others. My friend, storyteller August Rubrecht, always tells me, "Your music is better than it sounds."

In 1999, I was awarded a red ribbon at the Key West Conch Shell Blowing Contest for playing one pretty well after

15. Music for weapons and waste reduction.

demonstrating, "we don't have conch shells washing up on shore in Minnesota, but I did learn to play songs on stuff people shouldn't have thrown into our 10,000 Lakes."

That got me thinking about natural defenses. The conch shell is home and protection so the snail that lives inside can't be harmed by predators. Monarch butterflies and their larvae eat milkweed, which is bitter, and makes the Monarch an undesirable meal. We have biologists and environmentalists who know a lot about this, so maybe there should be more Pentagon study of this sort of thing to design our defense system. Watching birds led us to airplanes, and talking thru hollow logs began the journey to electronic P.A. systems. Why not a thorough analysis of nature's ways of protection without killing?

We had some of this with the medieval walled cities, designed, not unlike the conch shell, to keep invaders out. Of course, learning to go up in airplanes and drop bombs on cities destroyed that idea. After the massive World War Two bombing raids, Rothenburg, Germany is the only old walled city still completely intact, at least in Germany. They daily reenact a medieval story about invaders breaking the door down when the mayor rushed out and negotiated, "Look, if I drink a liter of beer in one gulp, will you leave us alone?"

Knowing a bit about drinking themselves, the attackers thought that the funniest thing they'd heard all month. However, when the mayor did it, the enemy army honored their commitment and left the city alone. Whether the story is historically accurate, or more a parable or blessing that helped Rothenburg survive, there are ideas in conch shells and walled cities that could be looked at for dealing with conflict without so much devastation to the land and the people.

FORTY-FOUR

I have a 1996 USDA Forestry report entitled *Do Trees Strengthen Urban Communities, and Reduce Domestic Violence?* The report cites a number of scientific studies showing people to be healthier, physically and mentally, in areas laden with trees. This includes healthy things like less child abuse and less need to rely on social services in times of need. There are also strong anecdotal studies of people in public housing, surrounded by trees, speaking of using reasoning more often than physical violence when in conflict with family members. The report suggests that having neighbors you can call on for support provides better ways of dealing with frustration than striking out. Places with nature and trees help relationships grow stronger so this can occur more often.

This was never a stretch for me, because anyone who's worked extensively with children knows the trick of, "If they're getting a little unruly, open the window or get them

16. Opening for FCC Commissioners and Captain Kangaroo in a smoke-filled room in the basement of the Kennedy Center.

outside and they'll settle down." When I mention this study, however, the reaction often is, "Oh, that's interesting." From others, it's more a smirk, and some comment, "That's ridiculous. Those two things don't even connect."

A few years ago, we began to see the studies suggesting that when we reduced lead in gasoline, rates of violence in cities tended to go down. Whoops. There are always lots of complex reasons for why things happen, but I've always told children the story of, "The best air in the world is in the forest, because when trees inhale, they keep the carbon dioxide we don't want and breathe out the oxygen we do. There's healthy air where lots of trees grow."

A lot of us are still struggling with some perceived difference between mental and physical health. People put on masks when the air gets so polluted they get sick, and we don't arrest people if they get a respiratory illness and pass it on to someone else. I'm not suggesting we shouldn't arrest people who commit violent crimes, but maybe planting more trees would lower the number needing to be arrested. Maybe our minds would all be cleared to think creatively on such issues. Maybe we should arrest more people who get wealthy damaging other people's health by fouling the air, or wantonly destroying forests.

FORTY-FIVE

During the first Gulf War, I was invited to do a week of day long storytelling residencies in Wisconsin schools along Lake Michigan. My work has always been to use storytelling and my *landfill music* to teach environment and social justice issues, as well as love of reading and writing. At the end of the day at the last school, I was walking to the car with the principal, whom I learned was the one who organized the schedule at all the schools. He was telling me how great the week had been, and all the wonderful comments he'd gotten from the other schools. As we neared my car, he said, "We must figure out to do this again soon."

Then I saw his eyes go to the briefcase lying on my passenger car seat, a bumper sticker on it proclaiming WAGE PEACE. I felt his body stiffen, and I suddenly realized that everything he had just said was deleted. "Do this again," was instantaneously changed to, "We'll never do this again."

About twenty years, later I was doing a day of SPEAKING OUT FOR WATER in a junior high in the Rice Creek Watershed area in Minnesota. I presented a number of environmental issues and then invited students to pick one and create a way to communicate need for change. They could create a poster, a bumper sticker or a story that might be delivered in public testimony to law makers. As I walked around the room, I noticed two students giggling about a poster in a way that suggested they were up to no good. I had learned over many years that quiet intervention kept such behavior from escalating and disrupting the entire group. I walked over and asked about their picture.

They explained, "The river is on fire," then laughed uproariously, clearly trying to not take me seriously, to see if they could push me over the edge.

I answered calmly, "Good work. That has happened a number of times. What words are you putting on the poster?"

Their faces dropped.

"Yes," I explained, "too often companies sneak out at night and dump really toxic stuff in the water rather than spend the money to dispose of it properly. There've been a number of times in the past when pollutants build up and rivers on fire are all over the news." Their entire demeanor changed, and the rest of the time they spent turning their meaningless joke into a serious piece of communication.

All of this made me think of THE NEW DOXOLOGY, a song I wrote, back in the 70s. I used it a few times, but soon put it away, unconsciously afraid it would get me labelled a blasphemer, unworthy to work with children. Of course, the real blasphemy is making a fortune fouling the earth, and being labelled some kind of saint because you donate to church or charity. The words are to the tune of *The Doxology*, or *Praise God from whom all blessings flow.*

Praise God, we've made our water slime,
The water Jesus once made wine.
Now we can walk on water too,
For it's so thick you can't fall through.

FORTY-SIX

Through my work with young people, I became friends with Mr. Khao, who ran the Lao Center on the north side of Minneapolis. Mr. Khao was also leader of one of the groups fighting for justice for the Laotian Special Guerrilla Units recruited by the CIA to fight alongside U.S. troops in Vietnam during the so-called Secret War in Laos. These troops were then trashed by some in their own country for fighting with the Americans.

After the war, they resettled here as refugees, where they were trashed for being immigrants. But the Laotian refugees built good lives for themselves thru hard work and entrepreneurial spirit. Now they're trying to receive official veteran status so they qualify for veterans' benefits. The difficulty is that there's no record they served. It was a secret war, so it never happened, though everyone knows it did. When the injustice of this is presented even to our most progressive politicians, the response goes something like, "I agree with you, but if I support this, I'll lose the support of other traditional veterans' groups, because they're also having trouble getting the benefits they should."

Mr. Khao once invited us to a presentation by Legacies of War, an organization raising money to clear the many unexploded devices placed along the Ho Chi Minh trail during the Vietnam War. The mines were intended to keep the North Vietnamese from heading south along the trail, but now, 50 years later, they are blowing up farmers and children who step on them. The Legacies of War speakers were young people, supporting themselves and their families at great risk by walking the trail with handheld devices to detect and then detonate the bombs.

After the event, Elaine asked one of the board members, a former U.S. Ambassador to Laos, "Couldn't the companies who made the bombs put up money for something like robots programmed to do this work? It would be less dangerous for these young workers."

Nervously, he replied, "Oh, uh, they generally don't like to get involved with these kinds of efforts".

Personally, I think they should, and it should be no secret if they don't.

FORTY-SEVEN

During the Iraq War there was an exponential rise of private security companies taking taxpayer money to pay freelancer soldiers considerably more than U.S. service members. Perhaps the most notorious of these companies was Blackwater, and one of the first flaps was Blackwater 61, a plane that mysteriously crashed in 2004, killing some high level military types, with little clear information forthcoming. After a number of company name changes, due to ongoing escapades, the owner, Erik Prince, moved out of the country.

Mr. Prince continued to receive U.S. defense contracts, and continually reinvents himself to do this kind of work in various countries. In 2013 he wrote "Civilian Warriors: The True Story of the Unsung Heroes in the War on Terrorism". In that book he claims, "All the stuff they've said about me and my company is not true. They're just picking on us because I'm a conservative Christian. The fact is that we can do it cheaper, and more effectively than the military". Mr. Prince also said that in the darkest hours of the attacks on him, he was supported and comforted by that other great, conservative Christian, Oliver North.

Oliver North is the former Marine who, during the Reagan Presidency, became the point person for secretly bypassing Congress to sell arms to Iran at a profit so they could send the money to arm the Nicaraguan Contras in their fight against the Sandinistas. There are still people who insist that money to arm the Contras also came from moving drugs from Latin America into low-income areas in the States. I know a veteran whose disillusionment with military operations began with having a friend whose military job was unloading those drugs from planes.

Of course, that apparently never happened because North summarily dismissed the drug claim as ridiculous in one sentence in his book, *Under Fire*.

When this whole thing came out in the Iran-Contra Hearings in the late 80s, North insisted that President Reagan knew and approved of what they were doing, and they'd do it again, as Patriots, because it was the right thing to do. Colonel North implied that Congress had its head somewhere inappropriate for not letting it happen in the first place. President Reagan claimed he knew nothing about the scheme, which led the process into a place where either the President was lying, or the falsehood stemmed from North and his Patriot Partners.

As usually happens with these operations, the whole thing kind of went away. In some large circles, Reagan was a great President and Oliver North a great Christian Patriot, who never told a lie unless it was necessary to save the Nation.

I just try to lay low and operate GREYWATER, a private security firm, telling stories to connect people with ideas, products, and services to keep their air safe for breathing, their water safe for drinking, their garden safe for eating, and their lawn safe for children to play or sit on to read great books. Of course, I also ask questions like, "Since we're now so concerned about Iran having weapons, where did they get them in the first place?

FORTY-EIGHT

When I came back from my all-expenses-paid trip as a medic in Germany, I couldn't get an interview with any local broadcast outlet. My dream had been to start a children's TV show where young people shared their talents, as opposed to just being studio audience, which is how it worked in the character driven local shows I grew up with.

"You don't have any experience," was a common refrain. Finally, in desperation, I took another youth work job in Austin, Minnesota, because I had a lot of experience running camps before the Army. There I found a new TV station just starting up, and they were interested in my show idea. I organized a club, as part of my job, to become a feeder for young people to appear on this local TV show. Eventually I tried to take the tapes, as they taught us in broadcast school, to the bigger stations in Minneapolis. No one would even look at them because producers were dropping local kids shows all over the country.

I had been taught to never give up. Having used portable video equipment with young people in trouble when I was in college, I decided to go back to school on the G.I. Bill to add a teaching certificate. I planned to use storytelling and video-making as prime teaching tools. To supplement the G.I. Bill stipend, I took an unrelated night job at Minneapolis Children's Hospital. Then, with the support of two innovative doctors, Karen Olness and Arnie Anderson, I started a specialized channel to help children navigate the pain of being in the hospital.

My big purple earthworm, a bit player on the Austin show, suddenly caught the attention of media everywhere. Talking with patients and interviewing their dolls and teddy bears on live TV became a big hit, and the show idea was promoted throughout North America and around the world. The free publicity, which celebrity types pay PR folks big bucks to get, solidified our funding, but it also brought other sorts of attention. In 1980, I was invited to do a workshop with Mister Rogers at a children's television conference in Washington, D.C. The only non-industry type there, I had to raise the money just to make the trip, unlike the well-funded PBS and commercial TV participants.

Shortly before this, I received a letter from Tom Root, a broadcast attorney, who said, "I read about your programming and think it's wonderful. My girlfriend works for the FCC on children's TV issues. If you ever need a place to stay in D.C., talk to me."

I made arrangements to stay with Mr. Root to avoid the cost of a hotel, and when I got to town, checked-in by phone, but never got an answer. We had confirmed my visit, before I left Minnesota, so now I was stuck. The moderately sleazy place I found to stay took most of the extra money I had. I tried, unsuccessfully, to contact Mr. Root when I got home, so tore his card up and forgot about him, until 1989, when I picked up the paper and read, "Tom Root, noted D.C. broadcast attorney, crashes small plane in the Atlantic and discovered shot in the abdomen."

The story was updated over several days, ending with Root, who survived being shot, under indictment for his work with Sonrise Property Management. Sonrise helped wealthy, born-again Christians invest in FM radio stations to bring the message of salvation thru Jesus to people everywhere. Because of the times, I wondered if the whole thing was some kind of front for running drugs into the country, but suddenly I felt I had been more safe in the decrepit D.C. hotel than I would have been with Tom Root. Root was later exonerated. All I know is that sometimes exoneration means nothing was wrong. And sometimes it' means you've got the best attorneys.

FORTY-NINE

Many children are still taught to say what we believed in the 50s, that, "Sticks and stones can break my bones, but words will never hurt me." But today we have more awareness that unkind words can be horrendously damaging. I think all spiritual traditions teach what is now backed up by much scientific research, that what we pour into our hearts and minds has much to do with what comes out in our actions. Still, when one questions the grotesque violence now common in too many video games, a common response is, "It's just a game."

Lieutenant Colonel David Grossman, in his 1996 book, "On Killing", details the discovery that, historically, a majority of combat soldiers became conscientious objectors by default. When faced with the prospect of actually killing another human being, they couldn't do it, often firing over the enemy's head to create the illusion of being a soldier, and to avoid the extreme penalties for not doing the job. Grossman then outlines the steps taken to remedy this, including use of extremely graphic video games, designed to overcome the stigma of killing the enemy, formerly known as another human being.

Back in the late 60s, when I ran camps for young people on probation, we had a camper who regularly delivered, with a fine comic sense, the line, "You mess with me and you mess with your life."

Some comedians have the ability to make ordinary material funny just by how they say it, and this young man was a master. About fifteen years later, I turned on the car radio and heard his name, a very uncommon one, in a news story.

It seems someone had messed with him at a bar in Shakopee, and he pulled out a gun and shot the guy. My former camper was on his way to prison. It wasn't just a game, and it wasn't funny.

FIFTY

Long ago, I saved an article, *Being Peace*, by Thich Nhat Hanh, a Vietnamese Buddhist monk, teacher and author. He said something to the effect that – *The peace movement has much anger and frustration. We write good protest letters, but we don't know how to write love letters. We must write letters to the Congress and the President that they would like to receive and not just throw in the trash. The way we speak and the kind of understanding we express should not turn people off. Can we in the peace movement talk in loving speech, showing the way to peace?*

I've experienced much of that anger and frustration myself, and I've always tried to write the love letter. When I was local president of Veterans for Peace, I wrote the following resolution, which we endorsed in January 2013.

> Be it resolved that members of Veterans for Peace, Chapter 27, will strive to refrain from derogatory language. We will treat everyone, no matter how extreme their opinions might seem, as someone with whom we could talk frankly, learn something from, and build a relationship with the potential to bring them closer to our mission of abolishing war. Further, in keeping with our Statement of Purpose, trusting all members to act in the best interest of the group for the larger purpose of world peace, we will strive to function similarly with the broader peace community. We will not allow doctrinal differences to impede our common goal

> of TURNING PUBLIC OPINION AGAINST WAR BY EXPOSING ITS TRUE AND FULL COSTS TO ALL. If we have a difference with someone, we will avoid derogatory mass emails, choosing rather to discuss such differences in person, with the intent of deepening our relationship and commitment to building a powerful, cohesive movement together.

The big slogan in the 60s was MAKE LOVE, NOT WAR. Too much of that was focused on unbridled sex, not necessarily connected with intimate love, but the slogan is still valid. King Solomon, supposedly the wisest man on earth, wrote the *Proverbs* in the Old Testament, saying things like, "A soft answer deflects anger; harsh words start a fight." (Chapter 15, verse 1, my own paraphrase.) He also wrote the *Song of Solomon*, a most beautiful picture of intimacy and ecstasy between love partners. If it is also a metaphor for God's love for his people, as some say, then even more does it show how to create a deep caring relationship between lovers, as well as between nations of the world. Thich Nhat Hanh is Buddhist. The Old Testament of the Bible is shared by Christian and Jewish believers. These 3 faiths, as well as others, all have a central teaching, stated as some variation of, "Love God, and Love your neighbor as yourself."

FIFTY-ONE

As a conservative Christian in the late 60s, I was drawn to Bob Dylan's *Blowin' in the Wind.* In various ways the song asked, "How long must war and injustice prevail?" When Dylan said, "the answer is blowin' in the wind," I sided with some creative conservatives who said Dylan meant the Holy Spirit. I still do, though I have a much broader view today of what that might mean.

When David Grossman reported in "On Killing", that military research discovered most soldiers were unable or unwilling to pull the trigger to deliberately take a life, I believe he was talking about the presence of the Holy Spirit, an inherent sense, not of cowardice, but of God, the Creator, the Great Spirit, breathing, asking, "How can you deliberately take life, which I have made sacred on the earth?"

I've heard the map of Minnesota described as *Up North* and *The Cities.* Dylan came from up north and began singing in the Minneapolis area, and his persistence made him important in the fight against the promoters of war. Many people here know someone who walked out of one of those early Dylan performances because it was so bad, but in 1961, Dylan went to New York hoping to meet a hero, Woody Guthrie. He did, and soon everyone in folk circles was letting the world know the answer was blowing in the wind.

Another Dylan song, *Highway 61 Revisited,* is less familiar, perhaps because it took a much more savage approach. The music has a string of violence and corruption moving out onto Highway 61, the road that follows the mighty and majestic Mississippi from northern Minnesota to the Gulf of Mexico. It ends with a gambler trying to create the next world war. The gambler finds a promoter who says, "I think we can do this. Just put up bleachers and make it happen on Highway 61." The war promoters are filling the bleachers and their bank accounts on Highway Sixty-Ones around the world. Let's come up with more persistence and better managers, players and cheerleaders, so we can win this one for the Holy Spirit.

FIFTY-TWO

Young people in the Occupy movement started fighting unjust foreclosures in 2011. At the time, I pointed out that the largest segment of the homeless population were veterans. When Occupy leaders asked me to speak in front of a bank president's home, as his bank tried to foreclose on a Vietnam veteran, I wanted something in writing on the subject of banks and war profits. I knew inherently that big banks make a lot of money during war because they're the ones who can make loans to gigantic defense corporations, but I wanted something systematically thought out and written down. When I googled ***banks and war***, I found a quote from Adam Smith, the 18th Century guru of free enterprise. Smith, who published *The Wealth of Nations* in 1776, made a statement so far from anything I'd ever heard, I thought it couldn't be possible. Suddenly I felt compelled to read his seminal text on free market capitalism, because I wanted to use the quote, but didn't want to pass on an extreme leftist misquote.

Toward the end of the enormous book, about 1,000 pages, I found the statement I was trying to verify. Adam Smith did in fact say, in the section titled *Public Debts*, that if war started, people should know they'd be taxed up front to pay for it so there'd be no temptation to go to war unnecessarily or continue fighting indefinitely. He also suggested, in *Taxes on Particular Profits*, that those who profit from the war-making should be the ones to pay the most. Under *Accumulation of Capital*, Smith spent some effort developing the theme that nations are more prosperous in times of peace.

So I wonder how many homeless veterans could be housed, fed and healed to the point of holding a job just by normalizing the excessive compensation of CEOs. Former Minnesota Congressman, Martin Sabo, tried for years to pass a bill expressing the following sentiment: *Pay your CEO whatever you want, but we're not giving you a tax break once it goes over 25 times more than the lowest paid worker.* Sabo, who died in early 2016, never got enough traction to pass the CEO-pay bill, and now the average CEO compensation is something over 250 times more than the lowest paid employee.

17. *11-11-11.* Eleven veterans celebrating Armistice Day by sleeping on the Hennepin County Government Center Plaza, and taking turns standing guard for the Right to Occupy.

I don't want the Draft reinstated. For one thing, I have 13 grandchildren. But I see the wisdom of those who call for reinstatement, this time drafting rich and poor, no exceptions. It's a little bit like taxing up front, so you know you have to pay. When we were young and facing the Draft, the necessity of thinking about war was thrust on almost everyone. To avoid this confrontation, those who instigated war in Iraq and Afghanistan, strategically drafted the National Guard and Reservists who were already serving. Everyone else was allowed to go about their business.

By the time the inevitable economic devastation hit, young people didn't know that war always does this.

They just knew they couldn't find jobs, had enormous student debt, and friends and family were losing their homes. At that point, it was easy to call upon the system that blames one party or the other for bad economic policies; meanwhile, the wars go on. I'm with Adam Smith. When war threatens, tax everyone up front, but tax those with the high incomes the most. They have the economic power to decide if it's worth paying for, or not.

FIFTY-THREE

We use the idiom *Sacred Cow* because Hindus in India and elsewhere won't kill cows even when people are starving. So now McDonald's is all over India, but they don't serve beef or pork because Hindus don't eat beef and Muslims don't eat pork. People are still starving in India, as well as in America, where we have other sacred cows. McDonald's franchising all over the world is perhaps one of them.

Fireworks on the Fourth of July are sacred. Americans gather everywhere on our Independence Day to celebrate the flag still waving over the land of the free and the home of the brave. Few are even aware that too many combat veterans quietly walk the other way, because the elaborate light shows of bombs bursting in air recreate the personal trauma of actually being in combat.

The Star Spangled Banner also poses as sacred music. Set to the tune of *To Anacreon in Heaven*, a bawdy drinking song, the difficult vocal range probably didn't matter when everyone was drunk. The inability for most ordinary, untrained voices to really sing along, however, seems unfortunate for the 1814 melody that would become our national anthem. Few are aware that the writer, Francis Scott Key, was also a slave owning attorney who used his position to suppress opponents of slavery. The words were written after a battle during The War of 1812, an endeavor where the British weren't satisfied with the Mission Accomplished aspect of the Revolutionary War. The Brits allied with the Native Americans, who weren't doing well with the Americans' new freedom to expand across the Continent. Two hundred years later, historians still argue whether anyone won the War of 1812, or if it could have been settled with better diplomacy.

We do know that Tchaikovsky got a famous overture, and that Jimmy Driftwood, a principal who wrote songs to interest students in history, became a famous songwriter. Driftwood's *Battle of New Orleans,* recorded by Johnny Horton, won the Grammy for Best Song in 1960, and became a big hit way beyond public education.

Fifty-four

I played in a junior high trumpet trio that did pretty well in the state music contest with our rendition of *Sugar Blues.* I actually played cornet, which is to trumpet as crocodile is to alligator. They sound and look pretty much the same, but cornet is shorter. Not too many years after we played music together, one of us was infantry in Vietnam, one in prison for burning his draft card, and one a conscientious objector, serving as an army medic without weapon in Germany.

During those junior and senior high days, I played *The Holy City* on cornet in church every Easter. I got up early to deliver Sunday papers, played the sunrise service, helped with the youth group Easter breakfast, then played the other two services, then had family Easter dinner before collapsing into the remainder of my rest.

I still love the song, its lyric using words from Revelation 21 about the Holy City of God on Earth, a place of no more tears, pain, or death. To me it suggests no more war – for, "the former things have passed away."

There's a bit of murky, non-evangelical Christian origin of the song, but I suspect it became famous in the circles I grew up in because Mahalia Jackson sang it beautifully at Billy Graham rallies. She also sang at the Martin Luther King inspired March on Washington, which I guess the people in my church didn't notice, as they were sure Dr. King was a Communist.

Someday I'd like to see a major concert where *The Holy City* is performed by the finest conservative Christian artists, back-to-back with the greatest peace activist musicians doing Ed McCurdy's *Last Night I Had the Strangest Dream.* McCurdy's lyrics show a mighty room filled with men signing papers that they'll never go to war again. The two songs come from philosophical traditions generally at odds with each other. Yet each speaks to a world where suffering and war have been eliminated. People can always find fine points to argue about, but who doesn't really want some kind of lasting peace? Maybe just those intent on creating a personal ***Heaven on Earth*** from inordinate profits created by perpetual warfare.

FIFTY-FIVE

In 2005, Elaine and I were asked to do a storytelling show on the local affiliate of Air America Radio. We had done several radio series before, but always on community radio where we just put the show together and someone else worried about finances. This was the first time we were also responsible for generating advertising dollars, so we signed a contract to do a monthly show, thinking that would allow room to come up with sponsors. We did shows around issues and the stories that drove them, always with a central guest-storyteller. We featured a doctor who practiced integrative medicine, a union activist, and others, including Mary Lerman, the amazing Minneapolis Park Board horticulturalist who developed the Peace Garden.

It actually made me think. I started the University broadcast program with an interest in international broadcast, but couldn't see how to make that connect to working with young people. When I was drafted, we used a little reel to reel recorder to send audio letters home. With the channel at the hospital, we helped patients in isolation visit with friends by engineering video exchange from isolation to classroom. I then started doing that internationally when Mary Schepman asked me to teach storytelling and video at the first Peace Site school, Longfellow International in Minneapolis. I taught children how to make video and invite exchange videos with Japan, Russia, Ecuador, and many more. Without thinking about it, I had fallen into doing international video with children.

Elaine and I won grand prize in the Tokyo Video Festival in 1986, doing a residency in St. Paul where we helped children create a video exchange across the Atlantic with a school in London. We were thrilled to get a congratulatory letter from Harry Skornia, founder of PBS, whose book,

Television and Society, was the only one I kept from broadcast school. He also gave us something I didn't know about, his attempt after World War II to create RADIO FOR PEACE, asking the best producers, writers, and talent to give their time to create a monthly special, so captivating it would engage people all over the world to do the hard, strategic work to build real peace and justice. That idea is still struggling to emerge, but we used it as a bit of a model for what we did with Air America.

The final show on our contract took place on September 24, 2005, the day of a massive outcry in Washington D.C. against the 2003 U.S. invasion of Iraq. We found a deal on flights and decided to do the show from the March on Washington. Our plan was to absorb the stories and feelings early in the day, then be at the start of the march, which fell right in the middle of the program. Our friend, storyteller David West, would be in the studio back home, and we would call with stories, first from the Lincoln Memorial, then the Vietnam Memorial Wall. Drop-out from our cellphones alarmed the studio engineers, so we compromised by collecting the stories from those sites, then doing the show from a phone booth in the basement of the Willard Hotel. This was the historic Willard where Lincoln maintained secret office space when he began to fear the possibility of assassination.

The March was enormous. The Minneapolis paper reported 7 buses going to D.C. from the Twin Cities, but people organizing in D.C. said 50 had arrived. We marched right by the Willard, but were so hemmed in by the crowd, we could barely get out, managing to enter the hotel just before staff quit letting anyone from the outside in. It was a crowded, classy phone booth for an hour, with the three of us sharing stories and music, including John Lennon's *Imagine*. The classic song was banned from many conservative radio stations, after the U.S. invaded Iraq.

We didn't end the Iraq War, but one of the stories that made its way onto the show was from the 1980s nuclear freeze era. Yale psychiatrist, Robert Lifton, met with a group of children, horrified because so many people were talking about nuclear holocaust.

One boy announced, "I'm not afraid."

Lifton asked, "Why?"

"Because," the boy replied, "my mom and dad and a bunch of other people are doing everything they can to make sure it doesn't happen."

Ending war is complicated, painstaking work, but fear is paralyzing. I want my grandkids to say, "I'm not afraid. I believe we can create a peaceful world, because my Grandma and Grandpa and a whole bunch of other people have been working hard to bring about peace."

FIFTY-SIX

I don't know if this still happens in conservative Christian churches, but when I was growing up, it was fashionable to give your testimony in this fashion: "My life was a mess. I drank too much. My parents got divorced. My best friend was killed in a car crash, and I was failing every subject in school. Then I met Jesus and everything became wonderful."

A thoughtful reading of the Bible indicates this formula to be faulty The testimony of the Old Testament prophets and early followers of Jesus almost always goes more like: "I started doing what God or Jesus asked me to do, and the officials beat me, threw me in prison and tried to kill me every chance they got."

Somewhere in the Psalms, David asked, "Why do the wicked prosper?"

Job, in his 21st Chapter, said, "Why do the wicked live, reach old age, and grow mighty in power?" He goes on to talk about their prosperity, but a lot of modern Christianity implies or teaches directly that following God's way leads to prosperity, usually meaning economic.

I am forever dismayed at being taught, by the military, that international law makes killing civilians a war crime. That's the teaching, but the practice has been slippery for years, and during the Iraq War, an administration claiming Divine Guidance began the same slippery interpretation of torture, another main prohibition in the Geneva Conventions. I'll leave it to God to make the final call on all this, but I know a lot of people are prospering by open violation of the rules we have set for conducting warfare. People who question it get treated like the Old Testament prophets and early Christians.

Last year, about the same time I got one of my regular

requests for donations to the University of Minnesota, they paid $150,000 for an hour long public talk by one of the architects of Iraq wartime violation of international law. I benefitted from my training at the University, but my career choices, working with children and young people, made me the kind of person capable of $25, $50, sometimes $100 gifts to causes I believed in.

My reaction to this talk was something like, "I made $150,000 once. It was toward the end of my salaried working career, and it took me 3 years to do it. If you can pay that much to somebody who was blessed financially for doing what the military taught me was wrong, why do you need my small help to lower tuition?"

The University said, "Don't worry. The money didn't come from regular operating funds. It was a private donor, and it's important to allow freedom of speech to this important person."

Well, then get the private donor to put the money directly into leveraging a mechanism to lower tuition costs, and allow the speaker to speak, for free, like most everyone else who exercises freedom of speech.

FIFTY-SEVEN

The work of Dietrich Bonhoeffer has had a profound influence on me. Most churches and people in Nazi Germany went along with the Hitler agenda, or conveniently didn't know about it. Bonhoeffer, a Lutheran minister was a leader in the Resistance Church. He strategically broke from a strong belief in nonviolence when he became involved with a group, some inside the military, plotting to assassinate Hitler as a best means to end the terror. They were, unfortunately, caught, imprisoned and executed shortly before the war ended.

I easily see how Bonhoeffer moved to the new position, but the difficulty is always *who gets to decide who gets killed.* These days, people on all sides of myriad issues regularly label their opponents as being just like Nazi Germany. Even without that, who gets to decide? It's hard for me to think of any kind of purity of motive in this, but I suspect there were some kind of strong feelings of doing the right thing with whoever really killed Martin Luther King, Malcolm X, JFK, Robert Kennedy and others. Governments, including ours, operate secret plans to assassinate dangerous leaders in other countries. Who gets to decide?

I got to my new place as a conscientious objector in the 60s when I discovered the historical fact that early Christians refused military service because of Jesus' teachings. I fudged on it by going into the military, but refused to kill, even though killing in a so-called just war had been acceptable Christian thought since the 4th Century when Constantine dreamed of a cross inscribed with the words, "In this sign, conquer."

Rather than asking if the cross meant "conquer" in the spirit of the original teachings of nonviolence, Constantine became a pioneer in the movement of Christian rulers waging campaigns of ***convert or be killed***.

A bit later in the 4th Century, Martin of Tours, a soldier, gave part of his clothing to a poor person, then dreamed Jesus was the person wearing his coat. Martin's interpretation was he couldn't follow Jesus while killing in the military. When he tried to quit, they called him a coward and offered to execute him. He volunteered to go to the front, without a weapon, and ultimately became St. Martin. Who gets to decide? Constantine decided for the majority, and gets more press. St. Martin decided for a few.

These days, most Christians don't care if the early Christians refused military service, and, in the words of Reinhold Niebuhr, there are far too many people "more concerned about swearing in basic training, than the war that put them there". For some time now I've felt I'd be moderately satisfied if Christians actually stood by the Just War Theory, since a main tenet states a war is just if no civilians are harmed or killed. Back in the 4th Century, civilians stayed home while soldiers lined up and killed each other. Since World War One, when we started dropping bombs and using other sophisticated weaponry, we've developed a system where ninety percent of the casualties in war are civilians. Still, we operate on slogans; we say, "It's a just cause," without looking at, or even knowing, the definition. If killing civilians is a war crime, maybe we should take a new look at how and why we wage war. Thank God, as I put the final touches on this work, the Pope is officially questioning the validity of the Just War theory at the highest levels of Christendom.

FIFTY-EIGHT

I got off the bus in Minneapolis at 4600 Columbus where, in 1931, Arthur and Edith Lee bought a home. The minute they moved in, the neighborhood was all over them, threatening violence if they didn't move out. The problem was, the Lees were black, and there was an imaginary line you didn't cross at 42nd Street if your skin wasn't white. The other problem was that Arthur Lee, a hard-working, respected postal worker, and a tough World War One veteran, was not accustomed to backing down. The Lees benefitted from the services of the first, and also tough, female black attorney in Minnesota. In addition, members of the Postal Workers Union and fellow veterans from the American Legion surrounded Lee's house to protect the family from angry, marauding neighbors.

Today there's a monument and a plaque at the corner of the yard commemorating the event. Arthur Lee is quoted on the plaque. "They didn't ask me to move when I was fighting in the trenches and the mud in World War One. Why do I have to move now?"

In the early 30s, when Congress tried to eliminate the possibility of making a profit from selling weapons and other materials during war time, the national political liaison for the American Legion was there to fight for the legislation. The Legion started in 1919 to help soldiers get the benefits they deserved, and apparently they believed there was a discrepancy between soldiers being asked to give all while many others back home got all.

It was 1934 when the President ordered the National Guard to drive out World War One veterans camped on the White House lawn because it was hard times and they still hadn't gotten a bonus promised at the end of the war in 1918.

Not too many years later, during the civil rights movement, brave African American citizens, with the help of some courageous whites, got off the bus and walked to work, at great personal sacrifice. They were determined to break an economic system that unjustly said certain people could only live, work and eat in certain places, and sit only in the back of the bus.

The question today is how to effectively *get off the bus* and get groups like the American Legion, to which I belong, to stand up to a system that sells weapons to both sides in a conflict. I do know I've always felt that if there's perceived need for war, weapons-makers should show the same sacrifice they asked of us – pay the workers to make what's needed, but no profit at all for CEO types or shareholders. That principle alone would begin to sort out what's really needed. But it is complex. The system making the expensive, obsolete bombers that never get used, or the weapons that end up firing back at our soldiers, generally also owns the companies making the food we eat, the busses and cars we ride in, and the media channels telling us it's all a good thing. I'm trying to find the door to get off this enormous bus and walk.

FIFTY-NINE

A church group once asked me to write on the subject of what it means to serve as an honorable Christian soldier. The elements are filtered thru these pages, but I'll summarize here.

When someone thanks me for my service or for fighting for our freedom, I respond, "No, thank me for fighting for the truth that Jesus says would make us free." Too much military action is so encrusted with falsehood, the real reasons can't be found. But an honorable soldier won't knowingly kill people so defense contractors and shareholders can increase profits to give more in the offering plate to make it ok. My own definition of Christian truth is that it's not ok to kill people, even in war, but if you accept the church's Just War Theory, or the military's Geneva Conventions, both forbid killing civilians. An honorable soldier will refuse to kill civilians, even if it means prosecution, as happened to someone I know who was prosecuted for refusing an order to kill "the enemy", a young girl.

An honorable soldier will pay attention to the Constitution for which he or she is asked to swear to protect from all enemies, foreign or domestic. I wasn't encouraged to read it before I was asked to swear. I did that later, and found the Constitution says the President can't declare war. Only Congress can declare war and appropriate funds for it. Framers of the Constitution did this to make it difficult to engage in an activity so horrendous as warfare. But most of our modern warfare, including Vietnam, was not declared. Most of modern war is therefore illegal according to the Constitution. I'm not suggesting an individual soldier take this on, unless he or she is ready for a bigger fight than going to war.

I am suggesting that all of us, soldiers and civilians, pay attention to it, especially when people pompously pound the Constitution as they send young men and women off to kill and be killed.

I had a first sergeant at Fort Sam who was one of the finest human beings I've known. He clearly cared about us as individuals, something that never seemed inherent in how recruits were treated by drill sergeants. I respected him, but I have no idea how he actually felt about war. In the chain-of-command context, there is no way he could have told me anyway.

When I was struggling with my own decision, before being drafted, a minister I thought I respected said, "In war you might have to kill people, but you may find children you can help." I still cringe at that thought, but I'm also conscious, in the horrendous milieu of warfare, of the example of the *Immortal Chaplains.* Four of them, Quaker, Catholic, Protestant, and Jew, were passengers aboard a ship torpedoed by a submarine in 1943. As the ship went down, they comforted and helped people onto lifeboats or into lifejackets. When it came down to the last lifejackets, each gave up his own for another. They were last seen holding each other, praying, and singing, as the ship sank.

Jesus said, "There is no greater love than to give one's life for another." Beautiful when it's done in that kind of purity. Disgusting when it is cast as related to the death of soldiers, unwittingly increasing the profits of weapons makers.

Finally, an honorable Christian soldier is part of the one percent of those who serve in the military. He or she returns with some inherent knowledge, experience, and courage that most do not have. I believe it is a part of honorable to stand up and keep fighting, whether it's for food robbed from the poor by unnecessary weapons manufacture, or treatment stripped from returning veterans.

We have a system that easily borrows money to fight even unnecessary wars, but is historically weak in care for those pressed into service, or those suffering because the economy was crippled by fighting illegal wars.

SIXTY

There's a group of stories, originally for adults, but generally popularized as children's tales, like *Sinbad, Aladdin's Lamp, Ali Baba and the 40 Thieves*, and others. The popular versions generally eliminate the overt sexuality, but maintain much of the violence in the way we so often culturally teach children to be ignorant of intimate love, while championing violent solutions to most problems. What's usually lacking in the popularization is how and why the stories were told.

Scheherazade was a brave young woman who lived in ancient Persia. Her King wasn't all that great in how he treated people to begin with, but when he caught the Queen having an affair, he lashed out in a brutal vendetta against all women. Systematically he began marrying young women, sleeping with them, then executing them in the morning. Scheherazade, knowing she would eventually be drafted, decided to enlist. She volunteered to go to the head of the line, and after enduring *marital rape*, she began a horrendous tale, designed to capture the sadistic imagination of the King. After weaving adventures to the peak of excitement in the early morning, the clever storyteller stopped and said, "I'm exhausted. I'll finish the story tonight."

The King begged for completion, but each night Scheherazade did the same, continuing her *tune in again tomorrow* tales for one thousand and one nights. Early in the storytelling, she began to build in educational elements of how to live in love and reign with justice. When she really was worn out after 3 years of telling stories all night, this courageous woman begged for mercy.

By that time the King, with benefit of an excellent education, couldn't begin to imagine his former evil self. The two were married to live happily, with liberty and justice for all. We have so many ways to tell stories today, but I think we rarely go for the Scheherazade effect. It certainly is time.

SIXTY-ONE

I did JFK's 50-mile mike in 1961. My college degree and draft notice arrived in the same day's mail in 1970, and I started writing this book a short time later in 1970. The Christianity of my youth urged the killing of godless Communists before they could take our God-given freedoms. I rejected the idea of a violent Jesus, signing on to be a medic with no weapon, willing to go anywhere, in my mind to get people back home where they belonged. Instead I was sent to Germany where we were mostly expected to stand around, acting like we had work to do. I threw my "book" away when I was discharged in 1972 and spent years, telling stories of peace and justice, but rarely thinking of myself as a veteran. When my mother died in 1991, I found a box revealing I had sent pieces of my writing home, I suppose to relieve my parents of the need to feel proud of me for "serving". This time I kept the manuscript, but it took another 22 years and the invasion of Iraq in 2003 for it to coalesce.

When I turned 61 in 2007, I hiked 61-miles, and I was thrilled when my grandson Tyler elected to walk with me. For him I think it was mainly an athletic challenge as it was for me in 1961. But walking that distance together gave us so much time to talk and to teach each other. My dad, an early inspiration for me to love walking, died at age 61. This hike remembered him, but more than that it rejected the lie that working for peace means, "You don't support the troops." I walked to say it is crucial to always negotiate every possible nonviolent strategy, and it is unconscionable for veterans who served in danger to still be struggling for care years later.

I also wrote, step by step, that too many veterans sacrifice needlessly, bravely giving all, while a protected minority make obscene profits selling weapons, too often to both sides.

This is the last of 61 very short stories, emerging from tiny pieces of paper, inscribed and hidden in my well-starched combat fatigues, 1970-72. They've spent many years being thanked for fighting for our freedom to "know the truth that the truth might make us free indeed". In the turmoil of the 60s, I began in a passive place of "pacifism", based on religious authority.

18. Card from my granddaughter Renee to celebrate my 61-mile hike.

During the many cups of coffee drunk while this book percolated, I've gravitated to the place of generating force, physical and psychological, to stand up to violence, always short of deliberately taking the lives of other humans.

The world's war-making has created a vicious, vitriolic circle, deserving of replacement by the circle of life. We turn former friends, or those we didn't even know, into "gooks" or "krauts" or "chinks" or some other derogatory label, making it OK to set out to destroy them or to turn them into homeless refugees. Then when they try to come to our land to rebuild their lives, too many of us try to keep them out because they might take our stuff. It's also worth noting that veterans still comprise a horrifying percentage of those labelled homeless in this country. They too are refugees from our wars and deserve the permission to come home.

The Good Samaritan in Jesus' story was one of those labelled the derogatory "other" of his time. I don't know how long a walk he was on when he stopped to help the injured man who was part of the name-calling class, but I walk to emulate him. I was trained as a medic, and I walk with the hope that all of us will strive to stop to help anyone, no matter who they are, injured on the battlefield of life.

ACKNOWLEDGMENTS

This book flows with acknowledgments, but here are more, not mentioned in the body of the book.

First, to my best friends in medic training, John Krebsbach and Dave Preloger, and to my current friends and colleagues in Veterans for Peace Chapter 27 and the Minnesota Alliance of Peacemakers.

The cover photo was taken by my friend, Gary Melom, Vietnam Veteran. The sculpture, *Walking with Birds*, created by another friend, sculptor, Doug Freeman, is on display in Decorah, Iowa.

Dan Tyson has been my attorney and friend ever since taking the first storytelling class I taught in 1978. His specialty is real estate law, but he's always involved in pro bono social justice issues, including the early fight for cable access, as well as affordable housing and legal support for artists. If he has a fault, it's looking out too much for others; not enough for himself.

The back cover photo of my Peace Bell was taken by writer/activist friend, Rob Ramer. In 2013 I was privileged to be one of eleven veterans/activists who worked with sculptor Gita Ghei to make our own bells in the spirit of the 1918 Armistice. Inspired by the long history of Veterans for Peace reclaiming November 11th as a day of peace, the activity was made possible by the voters of Minnesota through a grant from the State Arts Board. This, thanks to a legislative appropriation from the arts and cultural heritage fund.

My storytelling as activist work is inspired by my long, close friendship with Mark Wagler, force behind the creation of Northlands Storytelling Network in the late 70s. Mark grew up Amish Mennonite, and his "adolescent rebellion" was to become politically active with the Mennonites' historic peace witness.

I had already completer my 61-mile hike when Robin and Laird Monahan, Vietnam Veteran brothers, walked across the United States in 2010 to call attention to *Move to Amend* and their work to end Corporate Personhood. Of course, I sat up and paid attention to this important work to "get the stories into the hands of those with something to tell, not just big corporations with things to sell."

Amy Blumenshine, thru the ELCA, runs the *Coming Home Collaborative*, an inter-denominational support organization for church leaders to be genuinely helpful to veterans. Reverend William Berg (1930-2013), respected Lutheran minister, courageously went with me to the draft board to support my conscientious objection, 6 months before I was drafted. He said, "These are difficult times for all of us, and I support young men in whatever decision they make." I never thought of that as waffling.

Bob Milner, socially conscious businessman, first asked Elaine and I to tell the Sadako story at the now annual Hiroshima remembrance in 1982. Walter Enloe, former Headmaster of Hiroshima Intl. School and Superstar promoter of Cranes for Peace, is a close friend and big inspiration. Marj Wunder started the move to warn "No more nuclear bombs" at the Peace Garden, and JoAnn Blatchley works tirelessly to keep it going. Larry Boatman, fellow refugee from the extremely conservative Lutheran Bible Institute we attended, surfaced at the first Hiroshima event as a fellow activist in this work.

Finally, to Marieli Rowe, long-time director of the National Telemedia Council in Madison, Wisconsin. It's the oldest media literacy organization in the country, and I've belonged since broadcast school. I know my thought process is always infused with my immersion in critical thinking related to media.

Shipwreckt Books Publishing Company
Rushford, Minnesota
Purchase online at
www.shipwrecktbooks.com

Made in the USA
Lexington, KY
13 March 2017